Pádraig Ó Tuama is an Irish poet and theologian. Having worked in conflict resolution for many years, he now presents the podcast *Poetry Unbound* with On Being Studios, which has a____ssed over thirteen million downloads since its launch in 2020. He splits his time between Belfast and New York City.

@padraigotuama | padraigotuama.com

'Pádraig Ó Tuama is a bearer of light . . . this collection [is] a testament to the rare fineness of feeling and understanding that mark his brilliant work' **Lorna Goodison**

'One of the most engrossing books I have read in recent years' **Stephen Fry**

'Each stunning poem has been so lovingly selected by Pádraig Ó Tuama and then shared with so much generosity and care . . . an essential selection for poets and poetry lovers alike' **Salena Godden**

'One of the best voices in contemporary poetry today' **William Sieghart**

'If you are looking for a read that will warm your heart, inspire your creative mind and renew your faith in the resilience of the human race, look no further' **Elif Shafak**

'A source of sustenance and inspiration' **Tina Beattie**

'Pádraig's way of finding language to describe the details and intricacies and the shades of grey of the human experience, have made me a better person, a better songwriter and a better artist' **Camila Cabello**

Also by Pádraig Ó Tuama

Feed the Beast
Borders and Belonging (with Glenn Jordan)
Daily Prayer from the Corrymeela Community
In the Shelter
Sorry for your Troubles
Readings from the Books of Exile

Poetry Unbound

50 Poems to
Open Your World

Pádraig Ó Tuama

CANONGATE

This Canons edition published in Great Britain in 2024 by Canongate Books

First published in Great Britain in 2022
by Canongate Books Ltd, 14 High Street, Edinburgh EH1 1TE

canongate.co.uk

2

O
BEING

British Library Cataloguing-in-Publication Data
A catalogue record for this book is available on
request from the British Library

ISBN 978 1 83885 635 9

Interiors designed by Tom Etherington

Typeset in F Grotesk by Palimpsest Book Production Ltd,
Falkirk, Stirlingshire

Printed and bound by CPI (UK) Ltd, Croydon CR0 4YY

MIX
Paper | Supporting
responsible forestry
FSC® C171272
www.fsc.org

Contents

To Krista Tippett
and Paul Doran

with all kinds of thanks and all kinds of love.

I pray for this to be my way: sweet
work alluded to in the body's position to its paper:
left hand, right hand
like an open eye, an eye closed:
one hand flat against the trapdoor,
the other hand knocking, knocking.

Aracelis Girmay

. . . in the end we go to poetry for one reason, so that we
might more fully inhabit our lives and the world in which
we live them, and that if we more fully inhabit these things,
we might be less apt to destroy both.

Christian Wiman

Poetry Unbound

Introduction

A poem is a difficult thing to define. What is it? It's a little block of ink on a page, sometimes five lines long, sometimes fifty. It's a house of memory. It's a clockwork thing you can carry in your pocket; take it out, set it to go, and it goes. Tick-tock-tick-tock, it says, sometimes rhyming with itself. Some poems are full of love, and some of anger; some poems remember things that shouldn't be forgotten, other poems fantasise about the future, acting as a warning for today. Some sound like a song, others like a story.

All poems use craft; careful choice of words, linebreaks, metaphor and form. I love these elements of poetry, but I know that such technicalities are not the only way to love a poem. Most people remember a poem because it reminds them of something: a grief of their own; a moment of love in their life; a decision they had to make; a time of wonder and delight; a landscape they had forgotten; a pain they carried. Somehow, those little clockworks get into the heart, and help it go, help it rhyme, help it in ways we can't define.

This book contains fifty poems. Fifty little doors opening up to the world of the poet. And fifty little doors to open up the world of a reader.

A poem is often made up of stanzas, and stanza is the Italian word for room. Many rooms are populated with things: a chair, a window, a mirror, a painting, a broken toy, the remains of a fire, the evidence of love or its opposites, a child's drawing, a forgotten report card, a scent that reminds you of your grandmother. The poems in this book form a series of rooms through which to walk where the walls have stories and the furniture can talk, rooms that invite in your person and your intelligence, your own memories, associations, fantasies, desires and pain. The poems are not designed to make your life easier, even though many of them will; they are designed to notice and observe, to take stock, to reckon, to breathe, to rest, to stir and work.

Each poem is introduced with an anecdote of how I've needed poetry in my life. Then, in the short essays following the poems, I write about the poet's craft and their choice of form, the way they've shaped language to do the work that I think is important to them. Sometimes I use recollections from my life to reflect on how the poem speaks to me. My hope is that the poems will intersect with the stories of your own life, too; allowing you to step inside, to notice what you notice.

The poems in *Poetry Unbound* speak to the variety of human experience, sometimes exploring common ground, sometimes not: in one, Hanif Abdurraqib looks back to his childhood, remembering when a friend's mother threw her wedding ring out of the window of a car after the end of a marriage. In the background of this memory is a song in which the poet recognises his own grief. Maybe I shouldn't say a poem is a door between two rooms. Maybe it's twenty doors: what it means to remember yourself as a teenager; what it means to be an adult; what music works in us; how grief is a complicated ghost; how a crowd of friends crammed in the back seat of the car is a whole world.

Gail McConnell's poem 'Worm' is not written about a worm, but *to* one, the 'you' of the poem. I never knew I'd need a poem to a worm, but I do, because through this poem, I understand that the worm has learned to ingest everything it comes across. It goes through. It makes life in underground places. Us too.

Poetry Unbound contains poems about prayer, pain and power: Faisal Mohyuddin's 'Prayer' calls God a 'perfect / emptiness'; Lorna Goodison's 'Reporting Back to Queen Isabella' imagines a roomful of colonialists who imagined themselves as explorers; Leanne O'Sullivan's 'Leaving Early' is in the form of a letter from a woman to her husband – she's leaving him in the hospital for a night, going home, entrusting him to the care of a beloved nurse. Reginald Dwayne Betts's 'Essay on Reentry' is also set in the middle of the night: a man and his sleepless son watch cartoons with the sound turned down, a complicated conversation looming between them.

Some poems address huge topics: history, seeking asylum, religion, war, grief, ecology. Other poems are from a small corner of a poet's life: meeting a stranger on a street, making bread, self-forgiveness. Some address themes of abandonment, or remember a friendly animal. Poetry is about the human condition: everything from the kitchen drawer to the state of the world can be subject matter for a poem.

The poets in *Poetry Unbound* are from many places – Jamaica, Ireland, the United States, Australia, Iran, Puerto Rico, England, Israel. Included are poets from the diaspora, colonised countries, occupied countries, poets in exile, poets who have never travelled much, and poets who've been forced to travel to – or through – many places. Many of the poets hold more than one national identity. There is no such thing as one global universal voice. We contain multitudes, as Walt Whitman asserted.

I chose these fifty poems because together they help us to see what can happen when we pay attention to our lives. They are mostly from living poets; some at the start of their publishing career, others well-published. All the poems are a testament to the process of noticing. A single moment can open a door to an experience that's bigger than the single moment might imply. Sometimes that opening is a challenge, sometimes it's a comfort, other times a question. Very occasionally it's an answer.

The voice in a poem isn't necessarily the voice of the poet, nor is the scene being described necessarily true to life. Poets take imaginative leaps, and the experiences they write about are not always based on their own lives. Hence, I refer to the voice as 'the speaker' when I write about the speaking voice in individual poems. Patience Agbabi, for instance, speaks in the voice of the patriarch Isaac. It's a personal poem. It's not the poet, but it's not *not* her either; she's in control of the speaking voice, or perhaps the voice is in control of her. Often this kind of poem is called a persona poem. In other poems, the speaking voice seems more direct, closer to that of the poet themselves. The line between writer and speaker is a border, and permits many crossings.

Linebreaks, metaphor, form, word-choice – all are vital to a poem, and in every essay that accompanies the poem I make some reference to how the poet uses these tools of the craft to shape their art. But deeper than the *craft* of poetry is the *why* of poetry. Why did the poet write this? Or, perhaps, why did the poet *need* to write this? The poet needed to make a record. It's evidence of their existence: like our ancestors' handprints on the wall of a cave, an 'I am here'.

I've needed every poem gathered here and, in my brief essay that accompanies each poem, I articulate the reasons they mean so much to me. The poems have become like friends I turn to and return to. I admire the years of work that go into a poet's artistry. I know, too, that once a poem is released it develops its own life. It's a generous act, and a risky one, too. I find in a poem stories from my own life, stories of my friends' lives, losses and pains and joys reflected. I see the range of imagination, or limitation, or hope. Every single one of the poems included has made me more attentive to being human, ways of offering comfort, or challenge, or questioning. The poems turn to me as I turn to them. I am confident they'll turn towards you too.

I've worked in conflict resolution for about twenty years, focusing particularly on the ongoing legacy of British–Irish conflict in the north of Ireland. Themes of religion, language, citizenship, peace and violence have been part of my working life; I find a lot of those ideas in the poems I've selected. You, your own life, will find other things. This is the work of the poem, too: it looks back as you look at it. Your reading of the poem might change with repeated readings. My advice? Write notes in the margins.

The contents are arranged to resemble an exploration. The opening poems consider what self-acceptance looks like, knowing that memory, story, comfort, friendship and love are irreplaceable in the life of a person. Ada Limón's 'Wonder Woman' and Kei Miller's 'Book of Genesis' praise moments where love is found in unexpected places. Then the poems shift towards empowerment, reclaiming what has been threatened: a history, a past, safety, name, land and independence. There are poems of self-reckoning and poems of empire-reckoning. Natasha Trethewey meditates on miscegenation and Mississippi, Raymond Antrobus's poem is compiled of thirty questions asked of him by an immigration officer, Yousif Quasmiyeh's experiences as a Palestinian growing up in the Baddawi refugee camp open up the worlds present in a single square kilometre. Next are poems that seek to reconcile identity; Jónína Kirton seeks a metaphor that will help her hold her joint Indigenous and Icelandic heritages together, Faisal Mohyuddin fuses language and space to describe prayer. Included are many poems that consider parenthood and family. Martín Espada mourns his father; Carlos Andrés Gómez writes of becoming one; Marie Howe remembers and blesses her mother's body. Finally, the poems return to the self: in peace, in conflict, in abandonment, self-consciousness, joy and resilience: R. A. Villanueva places self-acceptance alongside self-conscious-ness and Aimee Nezhukumatathil writes a letter to her child-self, standing in a new classroom, finding her feet, shoring herself up with memories of nature and love.

The poems collected in this anthology ask essential ques-tions about how to thrive in a complicated world, about how to love when life hasn't been easy. Some are about navi-gating change, about celebrating one's self. The title, *Poetry Unbound*, expresses the idea that poetry's geography is one of exploration. Emily Dickinson once said that a good poem should take the top of your head off. *Poetry Unbound* releases the poem from the myth that poems are always academic, that they aren't about real life. These poems show how wild and free the world of poetry is, turning its attention to what is essential. Poetry *unbound* – from stultifying school examinations, from limited imagination – shows us the unlimited possibilities of what art can do. A poem can be like a flame: helping us find our way, keeping us warm.

Poetry Unbound began with a podcast initiated by the American broadcaster Krista Tippett, who founded the On Being Project. We've been friends for years and bonded over our mutual appreciation of poetry. 'Sometimes it hurts to read a poem,' she's said on many occasions. In my work in conflict resolution, I'd always included poetry: sometimes writing poems to help myself recover from a difficult case, often bringing a poem to a mediation to help folks consider how the poem could reframe the divisive issues in the room. Krista had always been interested in how I used poetry to speak to the everyday situations that affect us, and she asked if I'd like to run a poetry podcast for On Being. I said yes. She wanted me to shape the podcast to be interactive, where the audience could feel listened to as much as listening. A team of us worked together to make a podcast that would bring poetry to an audience, by hearing the poems read, and by my interaction with them. We wanted to create community and hospitality, to offer insight, to challenge, to invite curiosity. The first season of Poetry Unbound launched in early 2020, while coronavirus was in the news, but before any lockdowns had begun. We hoped for thirty thousand downloads, and instead exceeded a million that first season. And many listeners have written to us, telling us how Poetry Unbound has been included in their lives, telling us their stories about their appreciation for a particular poem and how it helped or inspired. Five seasons and seven million downloads later, we continue to listen and learn.

Perhaps you've loved poetry but haven't known where to start. Perhaps you've wanted to try your hand at having a conversation with a poem. Perhaps the sheer choice of what to read overwhelms you, or you're burdened by the memories of school examinations that seemed to flatten the life of any poem. These poems are for you: to read when you can't sleep, to learn and recite on a bus or train journey, to bring into a classroom, to accompany you in a crisis, to offer to a friend.

When a poem lands in your life, it really lands, adding new richness and texture to your world. I know of no greater gift than when someone tells me they turned to a poem of mine or a poem by another poet during a time of importance, or an occasion, a funeral, a wedding, an anniversary. I consider myself lucky, now, to stand at the doorway to this anthology, saying hello, inviting you to greet these brilliant poems with stories of your own. The poems are eager to meet you, too.

I've had a Wonder Woman belt buckle for the last ten years. Often, people have asked: 'Do you wear it because you need the strength?' Mostly I wear it because I like it. But also I wear it because growing up, the message was that boys shouldn't be interested in Wonder Woman.

But I adored her. Comic book characters are silly, in a certain sense, but not entirely. They reveal us; they reveal the imagination, notions of power, of possibility, of how to live in constraint.

Wonder Woman
Ada Limón

Standing at the swell of the muddy Mississippi
after the urgent care doctor had just said, *Well,*
sometimes shit happens, I fell fast and hard
for New Orleans all over again. Pain pills swirled
in the purse along with a spell for later. It's taken
a while for me to admit, I am in a raging battle
with my body, a spinal column thirty-five degrees
bent, vertigo that comes and goes like a DC Comics
villain nobody can kill. Invisible pain is both
a blessing and a curse. *You always look so happy*,
said a stranger once as I shifted to my good side
grinning. But that day, alone on the riverbank,
brass blaring from the Steamboat Natchez,
out of the corner of my eye, I saw a girl, maybe half my age,
dressed, for no apparent reason, as Wonder Woman.
She strutted by in all her strength and glory, invincible,
eternal, and when I stood to clap (because who wouldn't have),
she bowed and posed like she knew I needed a myth –
a woman, by a river, indestructible.

Ada Limón is a cinematic poet – you can often *see* what's happening. In this poem she's in New Orleans and she's come to stand at the swell of the Mississippi having just been to visit a doctor. There she is, a woman by a river, in a 'raging battle / with my body'.

Pain is everywhere in this poem: there's whatever required the trip to urgent care; pain pills that function for now and also as a 'spell for later', anticipating that the pain will return; there's that battle with the body; there's vertigo. Even deeper than a visible source of pain, there's 'invisible pain' – and the inevitable comments from people who are going to say, *Well, you don't look sick to me*.

Anybody who has lived with chronic illness will know that not only must you learn to live with your own symptoms, but you must also learn to live with other people's opinions about your symptoms: whether your illness is valid or not; whether you should or shouldn't take this medication or that; what will help; what will not help; whether the illness is your fault; whether you're believed or not. This is a burden on top of your body's burdens. Living with people's readings – people's moral readings, really – about your pain can make everything worse.

This poem is populated with people. The doctor, for whose pragmatic '*sometimes shit happens*' I have deep affection, and that stranger who says '*You always look so happy*'. Both of these characters speak, one with lack of certitude, the other with oppressive certitude. But it's the silent character – that magnificent girl in the costume – whose communication is most effective, replacing language with poise, power and mythology. In a certain sense, the poem's speaker has been yearning for someone to come alongside her and help, actually help, and while the doctor's honesty is better than lies, it's not helping much. The stranger is clumsy. Who can help when you feel so alone? The poem answers: a girl in a costume.

Wonder Woman is a mythological character, a fictional superhero from DC Comics. Superhero language is echoed elsewhere the poem, with vertigo being described as a 'villain nobody can kill'. Important to remember is that a myth is not something false, rather a myth is something with so much truth that it needs a fantastical container. In a poem with many real people, perhaps it was only a mythological character who could uplift her. So when, at the end of the poem, this girl arrives, she's not from the world of adults, or mere mortals – she's from a world of her own. Who is this girl? Why is she dressed as Wonder Woman? And does she act like a superhero because she's dressed as one, or is she dressed as one because she acts like one? What is her power?

I know that poetry lessons in school sometimes are a mixed bag of memories. But many people will remember the word *alliteration* from those days: where two words in a poem – either right next to each other or, maybe, just near each other – start with the same letter. 'Wonder Woman' is a perfect example, both in its title and in the body of the poem: 'muddy Mississippi'; 'sometimes shit happens'; 'fell fast'; 'Pain pills'; 'battle with my body'; 'pain is both blessing'; then, 'said a stranger'; 'good side grinning'; 'brass blaring'; 'strutted . . . strength' and 'knew I needed'. This entire poem is peppered, deliciously, with alliteration. Once you see it you can't unsee it. Alliteration is not just cleverness, however: Ada Limón uses the myth of Wonder Woman with the technique of alliteration to tell the reader we are not alone. Two words standing alongside each other; two women too. In the alliterative and comforting language of her own poetry, and in the myth of the superhero, there's a source of power from which to draw strength.

Whoever she is and whyever she's there, this girl in costume struts. The word 'strut' comes from an Old English word meaning to swell, to be puffed up. One of the origin myths of Wonder Woman is that she was sculpted from clay by her mother, coming from the earth, just like this girl. In Patty Jenkins' 2017 film starring Gal Gadot, Wonder Woman is bewildered by generals who don't go to battle but rather sit and deliberate in safe rooms far away from fighting. In the poem, the speaker is in a battle with her body – and with people's opinions about her body's pain – and she needs support. This is the kind of mythology the poet needs, and perhaps because she needs it – because she's looking for it – she sees it in the character of the girl. The myth of Wonder Woman in the poem is a myth about being a woman, in her body, sharing and gaining strength. Words like *strutted*, *strength*, *glory*, *invincible*, *eternal*, *bowed*, *posed* and *indestructible* are so often gendered. But here, Ada Limón searches for language, image and embodiment, claiming strength where it is needed, denying the projections of patriarchy and prejudice.

At the final turn of this poem, we're by the river, but the river has been turned into an origin story of its own: there is the girl holding all the attention, costumed, posing; there is the woman who, despite being in pain, nonetheless 'stood to clap'; then the girl bows 'and posed like she knew I needed a myth'.

The six words of the final line – 'a woman, by a river, indestructible' – always make me question who is being spoken about. Is it the girl now being portrayed as a woman? Maybe it's Wonder Woman, or a depiction of an everywoman. Or maybe the poet – in seeing this person who she doesn't know, standing in this costume and holding herself with such glory, maybe the poet *is* the woman by the river, indestructible.

It seems to me that the choice to place the girl and the poet alongside each other – alliterative humans – is to magnify the strength that true adjacency can bring. The girl offers no pity, and is in such contrast to those who offer cheap words, or whose sympathy is a further burden. She is doing absolutely nothing, but her costume and poise are drawing attention, and in receiving, she is sharing.

Through various ideas about whether there's a God or not, in and out of devotion, moving from certitude to agnosticism, the library of writings in religious text has never lost its fascination for me. It almost did once, but I accidentally began to read religious books as art, not authority, and the wonder opened up for me again.

Book of Genesis
Kei Miller

Suppose there was a book full only of the word,
let – from whose clipped sound all things began: fir
and firmament, feather, the first whale – and suppose

we could scroll through its pages every day
to find and pronounce a *Let* meant only for us –
we would stumble through the streets with open books,

eyes crossed from too much reading; we would speak
in auto-rhyme, the world would echo itself – and still
we'd continue in rounds, saying *let* and *let* and *let*

until even silent dreams had been allowed.

Years ago, Kei Miller came to give a reading in Belfast, and I couldn't make it. A friend went and raved about it, and I knew I'd missed something memorable. This poem is from the collection titled *There Is an Anger that Moves,* and more specifically from a sequence of poems that share titles with biblical books.

The biblical book of Genesis opens with a magnificent poem of creation, the one most people are familiar with, starting in most translations with something like *In the beginning, God created the heavens and the earth.* The creation narrative then goes on to imagine God saying: *Let there be Light!* and the response comes: *And there was Light!* Then, heavens and earth, animals and birds, fish and stars, plants and people. Each of these, in the English translations, is brought into being with a *Let there be . . .* followed by *and there was . . .* creeping things that creep upon the earth, swimming things that swim in the sea, speaking things that speak amongst each other. The average English translation of Genesis has almost forty thousand words. However, in his poem 'Book of Genesis' Kei Miller opens a door into this first book of the Bible with just one word: *Let.*

Let, Let, Let. When you read the original biblical poem of creation – or hear it, because it was written mostly for audiences who couldn't read, but who had a sophisticated engagement with spoken literatures – what stands out is that the writers esteemed language so highly they rendered it as the very tool God used to create the everything. In his poem, Kei Miller makes the logic of that 'Let' echo into contemporary settings: streets and books and scrolling.

'Suppose', he begins, and then imagines a book, a book full of one generous, world-creating word: *let, let, let, let, let.* It's a one-syllable word, a 'clipped' word, Miller calls it. And he echoes the biblical text, saying that 'fir / and firmament, feather, the first whale' might have come from that word. The alliteration is gorgeous, and the imagery too: a tree, the stars, the thing that keeps a bird warm and helps it fly, a magnificent sea mammal. We see the simple and the splendid gathered together in his lines. But in the poem, the word *let* is not just for worldmaking, it's for discovery too. If there existed such a book – or a scroll, he says, invoking both smartphones and ancient texts – full of the word *let*, then a person might search through that book every day looking for a let that would give them permission to be. If *Let there be light* made the light, then *Let there be you* might make a person feel alive.

With a book like this, the poet is saying, people would walk everywhere reading, stumbling on streets, echoing the sounds of that book in our everyday speech, searching for a sound that would let us be. If the biblical book of Genesis is about language, then Kei Miller's poem 'Book of Genesis' is about reading. His short poem imagines people scrolling through texts looking for something that's just for them. But it's not just imagination: walk in any city, get on a train, or sit in a coffee shop and you'll see people scrolling. It's easy to think that people are just wasting time looking at their phones, but this poem elevates the project of reading; imagining that every reading person is searching for the necessary – that *let* that will give space for their 'silent dreams' to be opened.

Insomnia runs in my family. My dad and a few of my aunties have 'the bad sleep' as we call it; my younger brother, too. I'd always slept well until I turned twenty-one. And then it started, or stopped. It's not always, just for periods of time – a month, or six weeks, perhaps – where I'll only sleep three or four hours. When it started it came at a time of distress. At twenty-one I was trying to figure out if I could – or should – tell people I was gay. This was 1997, and I had a summer full of sleepless nights. I was living in the northside of Dublin City. I'd wake at three a.m. and go for walks, often to Clontarf, out along a rickety bridge towards Bull Island and the North Strand. There's a statue of Mary on that strand, looking out across Dublin Bay. One night I stood under that statue and shouted, *Are there any other people like me?* And also, *I am so lonely.* There was nobody around for miles. I took off my clothes – I don't know why; maybe so I could feel as raw as I was – and stood there like some lost son of Eve, wondering if anyone else was alive in this strange suburb of Eden. Nobody answered. It was four a.m.

Reading Kei Miller's poem, I can remember that young man I was, shouting at the night-time for a *let*. And in his poem, I can imagine everybody that summer – those driving their cars, the people turning their lights on or off in the houses I passed, the bus drivers, the other early morning walkers – looking for a *let* too. And every night since then, every city, every town is filled with populations scrolling for a *let.* Looking at the world, Kei Miller imagines a kindness: that the deepest yearnings of the heart might be heard.

It can be difficult to be kind to yourself. Even writing those words, I feel awkward, as if kindness towards myself is a luxury. Sometimes a poem helps me to step outside myself and let some wiser voice speak back to me, looking at my own failures with clear eyes, offering understanding and compassion. This, too, is a certain kind of bravery.

Phase One

Dilruba Ahmed

For leaving the fridge open
last night, I forgive you.
For conjuring white curtains
instead of living your life.

For the seedlings that wilt, now,
in tiny pots, I forgive you.
For saying *no* first
but *yes* as an afterthought.

I forgive you for hideous visions
after childbirth, brought on by loss
of sleep. And when the baby woke
repeatedly, for your silent rebuke

in the dark, 'What's your beef?'
I forgive you for letting vines
overtake the garden. For fearing
your own propensity to love.

For losing, again, your bag
en route from San Francisco;
for the equally heedless drive back
on the caffeine-fueled return.

I forgive you for leaving
windows open in rain
and soaking library books
again. For putting forth

only revisions of yourself,
with punctuation worked over,
instead of the disordered truth,
I forgive you. For singing mostly

when the shower drowns
your voice. For so admiring
the drummer you failed to hear
the drum. In forgotten tin cans,

may forgiveness gather. Pooling
in gutters. Gushing from pipes.
A great steady rain of olives
from branches, relieved

of cruelty and petty meanness.
With it, a flurry of wings, thirteen
gray pigeons. Ointment reserved
for healers and prophets. I forgive you.

I forgive you. For feeling awkward
and nervous without reason.
For bearing Keats' empty vessel
with such calm you worried

you had, perhaps, no moral
center at all. For treating your mother
with contempt when she deserved
compassion. I forgive you. I forgive

you. I forgive you. For growing
a capacity for love that is great

but matched only, perhaps,
by your loneliness. For being unable

to forgive yourself first so you
could then forgive others and
at last find a way to become
the love that you want in this world.

Who is speaking to whom? I ask myself when I read a poem. The speaking voice of the poem isn't always the poet. Sometimes the poet might be taking on a persona, or adopting an all-knowing point of view: speaking to themself in the past, from the vantage point of the present, or the future. People write about the *speaker* of a poem, because every time a poet writes a poem, they give a shade of themselves a voice. Sometimes the speaker in the poem isn't the poet's voice at all, it's imagined, or conjured.

In this harsh and tender poem of Dilruba Ahmed, two selves speak to each other. Is it a mother self speaking to an exhausted daughter self? Is it a kind self speaking to a burdened self? How do they know so much about each other? We overhear a conversation between a forgiving self and a self that struggles with forgiveness. The speaker knows so much about the spoken-to, but unlike the spoken-to, can offer kindness rather than condemnation; freedom rather than restriction.

'Phase One' evokes the things we hold against ourselves, the things that prevent us from being loving because we're so caught up in stories of failure and accusation; some deserved, some not. There's a practical tone to the speaking voice in the poem: forgive yourself – whether you feel you deserve it or not – because without that self-forgiveness, things will be even more difficult than they already are, for you and the people you love.

What are the circumstances of the person being spoken to in this poem? They are tired, and then made anxious by their tiredness. They lose luggage. And then they lose luggage *again* (oh, the anger in that 'again'). This person has ideas of themselves – seedlings, library books, revisions – but even those ideas seem a dream in comparison to the demands of their daily life. This daily life includes a home, a fridge, a child, sleep, sleeplessness, a garden, travel, coffee, windows, showers and singing in the shower, self-consciousness, self-reflection, self-recrimination, a mother, a sense of loneliness, a voice that speaks wisdom, a mind that is looking for language that will work. It's a recognisable life. Seeing all the pressures spelt out in the body of the poem, it's easy for the reader to understand how exhausted the woman in this poem is.

The things I say to myself are worse than the things I say to anyone else. I'm sure you're the same.

In this poem, the word 'forgive' occurs thirteen times, and the phrase 'I forgive you' occurs six times. The first time, it appears just as a single sentence, just those three words: 'I forgive you.' And then the next time it appears in the poem, it's repeated: 'I forgive you. I forgive you.' The final time it appears, it's said three times, like a spell, a prayer, a hope, a song: 'I forgive you. I forgive you. I forgive you.' Little sand-wiches of forgiveness held between the *I* and *you* of a poet speaking to herself. This poem is practicing a mantra, in the hope that a life can learn that same mantra, and say it to itself, knowing once isn't enough; twice neither. What's needed is repetition. Once. Twice. Three times. Start again.

There's a reference to Keats' empty vessel towards the end of this poem. 'For bearing Keats' empty vessel / with such calm you worried // you had, perhaps, no moral / center at all', Dilruba Ahmed writes. John Keats was an English poet who died in the early 1800s at the age of only twenty-five. He suggested that poets should be *empty vessels* with no identity of self or selfhood; they should be like a container filled only with art. The speaker of 'Phase One' reflects on whether she could be that empty vessel, or whether she'd want to be, at this stage of her life. She feels empty, it's suggested, and the poem wonders what can fill the vessel of her life in a way that will lead to less exhaustion.

For many years I led a project that looked at forgiveness. I must have read hundreds of definitions of that word, but the one I keep coming back to is: 'not holding something against someone who has hurt you'. I liked the concrete imagination of holding something *against* someone. This can be yourself, too: holding something against yourself can be as demanding as holding it against someone else; someone dead, someone far away, someone you live with, someone you've never met, the self you've been. During those years of project work on forgiveness – I worked in schools and with churches and community groups in Belfast looking at what forgiveness might or might not mean – I found myself paying attention to my own lack of forgiveness. Some mornings, I'd notice that I was rehearsing an old anger over pre-dawn coffee, or in the shower. I'd come up with an argument that could finally put a nail in that coffin. But it never did. The anger never stayed dead, or buried. It always came back. Lack of forgiveness – for others, for myself – was something to which I was dedicating a lot of time, and in all honesty, it was its monotony that eventually confronted me. I needed to let go.

Compassion is more creative than contempt. Forgiveness – at its best – seeks to make space for surprise and the unexpected. That's what Dilruba Ahmed is offering herself:

space. Space to be tired, to take a break, to not waste hours in old repeated lines of self-recrimination, to be easier with herself so she can be easier with others. Forgiveness isn't the destination of the poem, life is, and the poet is aching for the capacity to forgive herself enough in order to be present for life without a litany of failures, hatreds and comparisons piling up around her. That brings our attention back to the title: 'Phase One'. This is the first step. The next step will be a little kinder.

There are poems I repeat to myself, almost like a hum, or a prayer, or a spell. I've said them so often they trip off my tongue. It feels like they've gone into my body. I know some people who learn many poems off by heart, and I keep trying to start up that habit again. I haven't yet been successful. So I return to the ones I've been repeating for years, again, and again, and again. They're comforts, a little bit of home carried in sound.

A Portable Paradise

Roger Robinson

And if I speak of Paradise,
then I'm speaking of my grandmother
who told me to carry it always
on my person, concealed, so
no one else would know but me.
That way they can't steal it, she'd say.
And if life puts you under pressure,
trace its ridges in your pocket,
smell its piney scent on your handkerchief,
hum its anthem under your breath.
And if your stresses are sustained and daily,
get yourself to an empty room – be it hotel,
hostel or hovel – find a lamp
and empty your paradise onto a desk:
your white sands, green hills and fresh fish.
Shine the lamp on it like the fresh hope
of morning, and keep staring at it till you sleep.

'A Portable Paradise' is the final poem in Roger Robinson's collection of the same name. It pays serious attention to the question of comfort, especially in times of distress. The book's opening poems are words of pastoral care addressed to the residents of Grenfell: a twenty-four-storey tower block in London, a building clad in material that didn't comply with building regulations. In 2017, what would otherwise have been a household fire caused the whole building to go up, killing seventy-two people. People had raised the alarm about the danger of that cladding in the years leading up to the fire, but the social housing authorities did not do the work, most likely because the residents were Black and Brown and working class and therefore not considered important enough to listen to. Even after this disaster, there are still residential apartment buildings clad with this same stuff. Inquiries are ongoing, as is the survivors' distress, and their distress about their distress.

So it is in response to these circumstances – in which Black and Brown British lives are continually put at risk and systematically ignored – that Roger Robinson writes 'A Portable Paradise'. The poems of comfort and consolation are written by a poet who's known pain to a population of people who've known pain. He's writing about how to carry comfort with you, no matter where you go – how to make a little bit of paradise portable.

Roger Robinson is a Trinidadian poet who has moved back and forth between London and Trinidad, so he's made home in a few places. Place can be a memory holder for paradise or pain. Paradise is a word that came into Latin and Greek and English through an early Iranian language, Avestan, the language of the scriptures of Zoroastrianism. The word originally meant 'an enclosed garden': perhaps the Garden of Eden might come to mind, or John Milton's epic poem *Paradise Lost* depicting Adam and Eve being expelled from that garden of perfection. Often, paradise is written about as an ideal, lost in the dreams and mists of time. This depiction of paradise, however, is located in the everyday, not imagining a *before* or a *hereafter,* but imagining the *here* with all the comfort and generosity it needs towards those for whom *here* has been a place of pain.

Paradise, for Roger Robinson, is found in a shell held inside your pocket, or in the piney scent of a handkerchief, or in the music you keep in your ears. In his poem the paradise needs to be portable because there are people who wish to steal it; 'carry it always / on [your] person, concealed', his grandmother warns him. The word *concealed* is often used as a weapon against Black and Brown people in London, with police and newspaper headlines accusing, stereotyping and criminalising those populations by practice and policy. Roger Robinson's grandmother knows that the stresses of the world can be 'sustained and daily' – big societal problems, as well as the daily worries of life – and here, we have a testament of how her grandson bears witness to her wisdom, keeping a private stash of paradise 'so / no one else would know it but me'. Her voice is loving, and long-lived.

The poem flows: the repeated 'e' sounds in *speak, speaking, me, concealed*, and *steal* is a poetic device known as assonance. How do you notice assonance? One way is by reading the poem aloud. The trusty *Princeton Companion to Poetry and Poetics* makes the point that you can't train a computer to recognise these subtle little rhymes. They depend on how a person speaks, on their pronunciation, on their dialect. Assonance calls for a person to hear themselves as they say a poem, which in turn leads them to hear a certain music.

A poem can issue many invitations, particularly invitations to identify with a character. A person might identify with the speaking voice of this poem, or with the grandmother. Someone might read something and see their lives open. In bringing my full self to read Roger Robinson's poem, I want to honour the part of me that's suffered, but I can't pretend I'm ever going to read this poem as anything other than a white man. Therefore, I ask myself what behaviours I've been part of that have taken other people's paradises, requiring them to seek shelter from me.

This is a seventeen-line poem, and the sixth line – 'that way they can't steal it, she'd say' – is a hinge-point, a place where the poem turns. Sometimes a poem turns in order to look back on itself, other times to change focus or subject. Here, at the turn, the poem's voice changes. Where in the first six lines we hear a first-person voice – 'if I speak'; 'told me' – the rest of the poem is an address, a list of instructions, a voice that speaks in an urgent and protective imperative. 'If life puts you', 'your breath', 'get yourself'. 'You' or 'your' or 'yourself' is echoed nine times after the turn. Who is speaking? I like to think it's the grandmother, or the echo of the grandmother's voice in her grandson. Who is being addressed? Someone whose paradise is under threat. Someone who needs to find a safe place to hide. This poem invites readers to recognise their own reality: a reality that others wish to bruise or steal or break.

My friend Dani would sometimes go to her housemate's room and nap in her bed. Her housemate would be writing a letter, or tidying, or moving quietly around the room; all the while Dani would be asleep in her friend's bed. I called round once and saw her. I was so moved that a person would say – with their body, with their tiredness – *it's safe to rest near you*. By knowing the experience of needing to guard your paradise – and knowing that your grandmother knew this too, so much so that she gave you advice on how to keep it safe – this poem of Roger Robinson's makes an audience for itself. And then it issues instructions: feel your paradise's ridges with your fingers; smell it; hum it; get to a safe room, light a little light and look at your paradise on the desk; stare at it, keep staring at it until you sleep.

The first poem I wrote was an idiotic one about a ten-foot dog. I was twelve. In the interests of making the poem rhyme, I put verbs at the end of sentences. Awful as it was, I was thrilled by the experience of creating something. I knew it needed improvement, but it was my work, and it felt electric. A poem about an oversized dog was just a piece of fantasy, a piece of silliness, a piece of play. The poem's long gone now, but I still remember one line: *he wonders if through any door he'll fit*. The huge dog's name was Tiny: something unexpected; something contradictory – a loneliness at the heart of things, wondering if he'd ever belong. I didn't think I was writing about me.

Worm

Gail McConnell

Burrowing in your allotted patch you
 move through the dark, muscles contracting one by one

in every part, lengthening and shortening
 the slick segmented tube of you, furrows in your wake.

Devising passages for water, air,
 you plot the gaps that keep the structure from collapse.

Dead things you know. Plants and creatures both.
 Your grooves shift matter, sifting as you go.

Eyeless, your appetite aerates.
 Eating the world, you open it.

You ingest to differentiate.
 Under the foot-stamped earth, you eat into a clot

of leaf mould, clay and mildew, and express what you can
 part with, as self-possessed as when you started.

Your secretions bind the soil,
 your shit enriches it. How things lie

now will be undone, will reoccur. You, a surface-level archivist
 sensing all there is

can be gone through. The body borne
 within its plot.

I studied Biology for my final exams in secondary school, and worms were on the curriculum. I remember drawing extensive diagrams of earthworms, the map of their innards imprinted on my mind from dissections, and copying words like *Lumbricina* into the graphed paper of my wine-coloured science notebook. Despite never doing anything scientific after school – to the dismay of my parents who believed science and industry were the only two pathways to a proper job – I've remembered details of the earthworm. I recall learning about the vast population of them; the importance of them. So when I read this poem of Gail McConnell's in her pamphlet *Fourteen* I was thrilled with the details of it.

A worm is a tube-shaped beast, made up of segments, with no limbs, no eyes, and no lungs. It has a mouth, a body along which its digestive tract runs, some veins, and blood-vessels – five of which double as pseudo-hearts – and it has an anus. As the poem suggests, the worm moves by lengthening and shortening its body. By tunnelling in this way, it makes passages that allow air and water and drainage through soil. Worms move through the earth with extraordinary force. It's estimated that, taking its bodyweight into consideration, an adult earthworm can exert a force of ten times its mass; and a baby worm can exert a force fifty times that. The earthworm's excrement enriches the soil, helping growing things to grow, as does the mucusy lube it secretes in order to help it move. In 1883 Charles Darwin concluded a book on earthworms with the sentence: 'It may be doubted whether there are many other animals which have played so important a part in the history of the world, as have these lowly organised creatures.' The earthworm is your friend, science tells us, and nobody needs to feel alone: for every person alive today there's up to seven million of the tubular bastards.

Gail McConnell is one of many poets who sometimes writes what might be called *creaturely* poems: poems in close observation of a living being. A creaturely poem allows for the fact that the poem itself is written by a creature, about a creature. Poets who write about other living creatures also need to address the creatureliness, or beastliness, of themselves. The poem presents Gail McConnell in strangeness. This is a poet who speaks to worms as if she knows them, calling them *you*: 'Burrowing in your allotted patch you / move through the dark . . . the slick segmented tube of you, furrows in your wake . . . You plot the gaps . . . Dead things you know.'

Some of Gail McConnell's poetry concerns the murder of her father by the terrorist Irish Republican Army when she was three years old. He was one of more than 3,500 people murdered in the late twentieth century in the ongoing Troubles about Britishness and Irishness in the north of Ireland. So murder has been a part of Gail McConnell's life since she was a child. Once, at a reading, Gail recited a number of her creaturely poems – about narwhals, earthworms and seahorses – and then paused to consider why she was so interested in these beings. She talked about how she admires beasts who live their lives far away from light, and implied that she, too, had had to find nurture in underground places.

Knowing that, I find myself coming back to lines in this poem and seeing them in a new way: 'you / move through the dark' and 'furrows in your wake' make me think of phrases like 'the dark days of the Troubles' that you'd hear a lot in Belfast, as well as the practice of the wake after a funeral. The worm can 'plot the gaps that keep the structure from collapse' and I wonder what words like 'collapse' mean in a family affected by murder. 'Dead things you know', the speaker says to the worm, and, knowing what we know about her life, we hear a communication of regard from Gail to the worm. You can read this poem for the first time and think it's only about the worm; and then you can read it again and think it's about the art of survival; and then you can read it again, and again, and again and hear that it's a poem about the space between, about how certain survivals mean you see – and admire – survivals everywhere. The poem is surface-level, but not shallow. Gail McConnell *looks* at the worm, has researched it, shown interest and curiosity in it. Inevitably then, and strangely too, a poem about the worm also becomes a poem about the poet.

It's worth looking at the structure of this poem with the same intensity that Gail McConnell looks at the worm. It's a poem of twenty lines, broken up into ten couplets of uneven length. There are twelve full sentences in the poem, going from the first sentence that takes four full lines:

Burrowing in your allotted patch you
    move through the dark, muscles contracting one by one
in every part, lengthening and shortening
    the slick segmented tube of you, furrows in your wake.

to sentences as short as four words:

Dead things you know. Plants and creatures both.

The lines are expanding and contracting, just like the worm; burrowing, making passages for air and water, holding it all together. These thirteen sentences are doing what they need to do to keep going, sometimes long, sometimes short, sometimes ingesting an obstacle, other times devising pathways around. The poem doesn't have predictable rhyme, instead establishing its own percussion with unexpected rhyme-patterns that happen sporadically, sometimes in direct echoes of each other, sometimes more obliquely. So 'patch' and 'contracting' pick up each other's sounds, as do 'gaps' and 'collapse'. 'Know' and 'go' rhyme, and we can feel the space being made in the rhyme established between 'aerate' and 'differentiate'. Each death is a new parting, so 'part with' and 'started' form an extraordinarily arresting kind of music, and then the rhyme of 'shit' and 'enriches' enriches us, making us think of everything that's left behind. Finally, there's the 'archivist' who senses 'all there is'. Who is this archivist? The worm, indeed; the poet, too; and anyone burrowing through the tunnels for the sake of their life.

Reading the line 'How things lie // now will be undone, will reoccur' in the context of grief, I find myself feeling relief, knowing the earthworm might travel through the same 'allotted patch' of soil throughout a life. All griefs will need to be carried, and revisited. There's wisdom in realising we are not undone by such revisitations. This, too, is part of being alive.

'Worm' is a pastoral poem in the sense that it might be set in a field, but unlike many pastoral poems, it shies away from describing nature in idyllic language. This is a poem of guts and blood, of slow, intuitive bodywork. The worm is 'sensing all there is // can be gone through.' I'm always struck by the verb *sensing*. We, like the worm, have to rely on our senses to get through: body memory, and one steady movement after another, can help aerate what might otherwise be suffocating. The message of the poem – not a rallying cry, but a story of how a body gets through – makes this a work of generosity and care. Survive with me, it seems to say, learn from the lovely worm.

Once, in New York City, I was sitting on a bench in Union Square, writing. A man came up and sat right next to me. He was tall and athletic, wearing sneakers and a wedding dress. He sat close, looked at what I was writing, turned his head to me and said 'Your writing's too small.'

Then he walked away. No introduction. No farewell.

Another time, also in Union Square, I sat and listened to Hare Krishnas singing for an afternoon. I love the music of that tradition. A man sat next to me. Anyone looking at us would assume we knew each other, but we were strangers. After half an hour, he said, 'Are you here because you need this?' I said, 'I am.' 'So am I,' he said. We spoke then, for a long time – two men in need – listening to the music and trying to figure out how to pay attention to our lives.

Wishing Well

Gregory Pardlo

Outside the Met a man walks up sun
tweaking the brim sticker on his Starter cap
and he says pardon me *Old School*, he
says you know is this a wishing well?
Yeah *Son* I say sideways over my shrug.
       Throw your bread on the water.
I tighten my chest wheezy as Rockaway beach
sand with a pull of faux smoke from my e-cig
to cozy the truculence I hotbox alone
and I am at the museum because it is not a bar.
Because he appears not to have changed
them in days I eye the heel-chewed hems
of his pants and think probably he will
ask me for fifty cents any minute now wait
for it. A smoke or something. Central Park displays
the frisking transparency of autumn. Tracing
paper sky, leaves like eraser crumbs gum
the pavement. As if deciphering celestial
script I squint and purse off toward the roof
line of the museum aloof as he fists two
pennies from his pockets mumbling and then
aloud my man he says hey my man I'm going
to make a wish for you too.
       I am laughing now so what you want
me to sign a waiver? He laughs along ain't
say all that he says but you do have to
hold my hand.   And close your eyes.

I make a starless night of my face before
he asks are you ready. Yeah *dawg* I'm ready.
Sure? Sure let's do this his rough hand
in mine inflates like a blood pressure cuff and I
squeeze back as if we are about to step together
from the sill of all resentment and timeless
toward the dreamsource of un-needing the two
of us hurtle sharing the cosmic breast
of plenitude when I hear the coins blink against
the surface and I cough up daylight like I've just
been dragged ashore. See now
you'll never walk alone he jokes and is about
to hand me back to the day he found me in
like I was a rubber duck and he says you got to let
go but I feel bottomless and I know he means
well though I don't believe
            and I feel myself shaking
my head no when he means let go his hand.

There are many reasons why this poem is brilliant and even more reasons to love it. I am moved by it each time I read it. Reading it, we find ourselves in a city, New York, outside the Metropolitan Museum watching one man who wishes to be alone and another man who keeps talking. It's a scene that happens every day. The stranger arrives complete, full of warmth and engagement. The poet is reluctant, gradually opening, reserve yielding to regard.

Why is the poet outside the museum? He's trying to smoke, and he says that he is there because 'it is not a bar.' So he's avoiding drink by going to the museum, but he's not even in the museum: he's outside, trying to be alone in a public place. The tension in the poet is clear; his location reveals it. Then this stranger approaches him and starts to talk: 'you know is this a wishing well?' He addresses the speaker as *Old School* – familiar talk between unfamiliar men.

At first, the speaker's responses are curt, short, suspicious; he's expecting to be asked for something, imagining that the chatty man might be homeless. Why is this? Because he thinks the stranger hasn't changed his clothes in days; because he assumes he's going to ask for money; because he wants to be alone and this projection is a way to keep the stranger at arm's length. What is the story of this stranger? We don't know anything about him, apart from the fact that he is perfectly himself, at ease with starting conversations, and not disheartened by the short replies of a man outside a museum. The stranger – we never know his name – asks if the pool they're by is a wishing well, and even though he receives a gruff reply, he still persists: 'I'm going / to make a wish for you too'. Does he wander the city sharing wishes with every person who's at the edge of themselves? The speaker of the poem is still committed to solitude: 'I tighten my chest wheezy as Rockaway beach / sand with a pull of faux smoke on my e-cig / to cozy the truculence I hotbox alone'.

Both of these men are alone: one edgy; one embracing. Sometimes I've been the stranger who assumes friendliness; other times I've been the friendless stranger.

Gregory Pardlo's poem captures the sounds of urban conversation and urban settings. The interaction between the men is everyday: overlapping voices, characters you'd recognise using terms of easy but uncommitted familiarity – '*Old School . . . Son*', shrugs, sideways conversations, a smoke. Fragments of conversations are interrupted by the sounds of traffic. All of this takes place with the feeling of autumn in the air, the roofline of the museum visible, framing the sky. This is a poem that places all of these noises and settings together, giving no guidance about how to read the shifting scenes, no punctuation marks for knowing who's speaking, where to pause, where to breathe – just like a city.

When the poem's stranger offers a wish, the speaker quips about whether he'll have to sign a waiver, anticipating some unnamed threat. Fast-paced language, shifty looks, surprising encounters – the sounds of a city – and yet, all of that fades to the background as our curiosity focuses on a singular wonder: What is going to happen? Will these two men become friends? How will this action resolve itself?

'[C]lose your eyes' the stranger says and the two men hold hands. Where's that solitary speaker now? Holding onto a stranger, hoping it'll help.

Isolation has evolved into touch. The 'rough hand' of the stranger

inflates like a blood pressure cuff and I
squeeze back as if we are about to step together
from the sill of all resentment and timeless
toward the dreamsource of un-needing

Suddenly, this experience of touch is an opportunity for the speaker to confess: his resentments, his desires, his desperation. He seems, in this moment of encounter, to be able to step out of everything that's restrained him, to have found the rest at the end of escape, and is now being hurtled towards 'the cosmic breast / of plenitude'. The speaker has been filled with his own longing and loneliness but suddenly, holding hands with a man he's only just met, they're both hurtling towards plenty, towards flourishing, through an encounter that feels like a healing.

'I cough up daylight like I've just / been dragged ashore'. What has this solitary speaker been drowning in? And what did this stranger see, so clearly? All the while we've been hearing what the speaker sees in the chatty well-wishing man, but here, we get a sense of what the stranger sees: a man alone, in need of a friend.

When the stranger says 'let / go', Pardlo shows how much can be achieved by a linebreak. The poem allows for space – an enjambment – between the 'let' and the 'go'. Taken just as a single unit, the line reads 'and he says you got to let'. Let what? Let life – growth, goodness, connection – in?

It's like an echo of the speaking voice in Genesis: *Let there be Light! And there was Light.* All of this achieved by breaking a line. The line doesn't stand as a singular unit, however, because it continues into 'go': go on with your life, go on with growth. 'Let / go' in this poem means so much, even the speaker misunderstands what he's hearing. Of course the stranger means for him to let go of his hand but there's also an invitation to let go of those resentments, of sadness, of isolation and the desperate fear of a stranger.

The title – 'Wishing Well' – makes me think of wells with pennies in. But wishing can act in another way too – to wish someone well. So this whole encounter could be an exploration of what it means to be wished well by someone else. The story of touch and surprise and plenitude opens up a well of longing, loneliness, and of a need that is met by the touch of this stranger's hand. A pressure cuff. A rescue. A reminder.

Often in a life, a person wonders whether they're alone. And when I say *a person*, I'm definitely referring to me, and hoping many others are with me, too. In wondering about aloneness, I often look for a text – a story, a poem, any kind of prayer – that can be some echo of someone else who is wondering what I'm wondering. In this way, poetry has become a conversational scripture for me.

All My Friends Are Finding New Beliefs

Christian Wiman

All my friends are finding new beliefs.
This one converts to Catholicism and this one to trees.
In a highly literary and hitherto religiously indifferent Jew
God whomps on like a genetic generator.
Paleo, Keto, Zone, South Beach, Bourbon.
Exercise regimens so extreme she merges with machine.
One man marries a woman twenty years younger
and twice in one brunch uses the word *verdant*;
another's brick-fisted belligerence gentles
into dementia, and one, after a decade of finical feints and teases
like a sandpiper at the edge of the sea,
decides to die.
Priesthoods and beasthoods, sombers and glees,
high-styled renunciations and avocations of dirt,
sobrieties, satieties, pilgrimages to the very bowels of being . . .
All my friends are finding new beliefs
and I am finding it harder and harder to keep track
of the new gods and the new loves,
and the old gods and the old loves,
and the days have daggers, and the mirrors motives,
and the planet's turning faster and faster in the blackness,
and my nights, and my doubts, and my friends,
my beautiful, credible friends.

When I turned forty, I was shocked by what happened. Before that birthday, I had always assumed people invented or performed their age crises. I'd tried it myself: *I'm thirty, my god.* Or, *I'm half of seventy.* But all of the year leading up to forty, if anyone asked me what age I was, I said *I'll be forty next birthday.* Something was trying to get my attention, but I didn't know it. Then I turned forty and actually, nothing happened. I was just one day older than the day before. But I realised, almost accidentally, that I'd turned a corner. I'd lived through my thirties – which felt to me like the first properly adult decade of my life – and at forty I thought, *I'm going to be fifty tomorrow, and sixty the day after that.* All those decades I hope to reach were opening up to my imagination. Sixty wasn't old; nor was seventy. It was just an age, an age I'd turn some tomorrow. When I was forty-five, my father, seventy-seven, said *You're now firmly in the realm of your mid-forties. Thanks Dad*, I said. I think he was trying to figure it out, too. This is one of the things that midlife has been for me: decades that once seemed old now just seem inevitable.

Christian Wiman's 'All My Friends Are Finding New Beliefs' is written about that vast experience of middle age, a stage of life that's not the same for everyone: some people change dramatically while others seem to change slowly, and others seem barely to change at all. In the poem, Wiman observes the friendships of his middle age, and, in a certain sense, considers the deepening differences emerging between them, both in life choices and life circumstances. It's a poem populated with friends: the one who converts to Catholicism; the other to trees; the one who tries new diets and exercise routines; the one at brunch in the new marriage; the one with dementia; the one who decides to die. Six friends, at least. My friend Daniel says that we all need five friends. When he says that he often also says 'I'll be one of your five.' He's a generous man.

In his memoir *My Bright Abyss* Wiman writes that when he began to be more open to belief, he began, also, to become more open to doubt. Belief and doubt are part of the same thing. If you're not interested in something, it doesn't matter whether you believe passionately in it or passionately against it. Nonchalance is not a posture of belief/unbelief; it's just disinterest. Christian Wiman's writing questions religion, meaning, what it means to love, and what it means – for him – to live long-term with cancer. He looks at the things that are hard to look at: love and its opposites; belief and its opposites; parenthood and its opposites; the thing and the no-thing. In 'All My Friends Are Finding New Beliefs' he looks at his friends with curiosity. It's a curiosity that isn't afraid – he names what he sees, especially things that are new, or different, or strange for him – but it's not a curiosity laced with cynicism.

'[T]he days have daggers, and the mirrors motives,' he writes. I hear some of my own fears being echoed in his lines. He's seeing threat in the passing days, days that remind him of age and a changing body. The first stanza ends with an introduction of new rhymes. A rhythm builds in the poem: 'Priesthoods' and 'beasthoods'. Halfway through the poem gains momentum like the speeding of time:

and the old gods and the old loves,
and the days have daggers, and the mirrors motives,
and the planet's turning faster and faster in the blackness,
and my nights, and my doubts, and my friends

With a mounting crescendo, you'd expect the poem to end with a killer line, something devastating, perhaps some recognition of the strangeness of all meaning. But it ends unexpectedly with the embrace of friends, 'beautiful, credible friends.'

'All My Friends Are Finding New Beliefs' could be the title of a satirical essay. But while this poem begins with what might be detached or amused judgment – 'One marries a woman twenty years younger / and twice in one brunch uses the word *verdant*' – it doesn't stay there. Wiman shows the crises of midlife, the different ways in which health, time, death, religion and choices land for different people, but then he goes further. He's not standing above his friends judging them; he's among them. He's not content to make comments which are callous, or sardonic, or clever; indifferent to the secret anxieties of people experiencing their own crises of time. He is skilled enough as a poet to know that skill isn't enough. He's interested in pairing skill with love, observation with commitment, bewilderment with dedication. And whatever his friends do, whatever peculiar choices some of them might make, those choices aren't enough to stop them being his friends.

You can hear anxiety in the poem. It brings readers to an abyss: the planet is spinning 'faster and faster in the black-ness', and oh, those nights and doubts. But alongside existential anxiety, this poem believes in friendship: the abyss is real, and it brings serious questions; friendships, too, are real, the stuff of survival, and what sustains.

There are certain poems I turn to when I'm in grief; and others that I avoid completely.

In the first shock of sadness after someone's death, I often need poems that remind me of what it is to be alive, or poems that echo the physical sensation of loss. The more I've loved someone the more empty life feels without them. But eventually, grief makes space for other feelings too. Gratitude returns: the gift of having loved someone – and having been loved back – doesn't replace grief, but it does accompany it.

Some poems help me as I mix gratitude in with grief; I'll treasure those poems forever.

Don't Miss Out! Book Right Now for the Journey of a Lifetime!

Imtiaz Dharker

We plan a holiday, a mini-break, a long weekend, a stolen week.
We trawl the options, seek out the perfect combination of hotel
and flight, the distant beach, the extra night, consider packing
suitcases, examine the travel clothes and lotions, get as far as
tying on our baggage tags. Then I look at you standing here
in this pale grey light and think that I have miles and miles
to go before I know you, and as in any unknown country
I may wish to travel to your sites, and make repeated
visits to become familiar with you. We look out of
the bedroom window at the usual view and think
we may prefer to linger on here, where we have
each other's endless landscapes to explore,
where I seek out your shore, you stalk my
tigers and the world will say it lost us.
This will be our stolen week, your
kiss my break, my eyes your lake
your mouth will be my Paris.
And as for Machu Picchu,
there are other routes
than dizzy altitude
to render us light-
headed, other
ways than
thin blue
air to
leave
us

breathless, and we are here,
not away not far but where
we want to be, still where
we were, this red arrow
pointing straight at
who we are, and

You Are
Here

Sometimes a poem's story is in its shape as well as its sound and syntax (*syntax* meaning words and their order; I said syntax because I love repeated S sounds; I'm a sucker for sound). So, thinking of shape, this poem by the British–Pakistani poet Imtiaz Dharker can be looked at sideways. Turn the page so that the left-hand margin forms a straight horizontal. What do you see? I see a large and gradual downward slope, followed by a slope that ends with a cliff and a gap and an outcrop of rocks. What are they? Ski slopes? Hills rolling down to the sea? Maybe it's a print-out from a machine meant to listen to the heart. Turn the page right-way up and look again: perhaps it's half a tornado, or a fragment of a ♥.

This gorgeous love poem is written from Imtiaz Dharker to her late husband Simon Powell, who died in 2009. They were both in their fifties when they married; he was already living with cancer, and died a few years later.

The title of this poem, two short sentences – 'Don't Miss Out! Book Right Now for the Journey of a Lifetime!' – sounds like an advertisement from a travel company. The exclamation marks at the end of each sentence add a note of urgency, or comedy. The poem begins with that kind of urgency too: with the holiday, the options, the accommodation and travel, the changed plans, the packing . . . Then, so early in the poem, there's a turn, and all urgency glides away: 'Then I look at you standing here / in this pale grey light'. The allure of a destination and all the busyness that getting to a destination brings are undone in this gaze, right on the cusp of departure. In the lines 'think that I have miles and miles / to go before I know you' Imtiaz Dharker echoes Robert Frost's line: 'And miles to go before I sleep'. But her poem celebrates arrivals: instead of unreachable destinations, the lovers reach for each other; instead of unknown lands they have 'each other's endless landscapes to explore'. Wherever they could have gone – a lake, Paris, Machu Picchu – they have other ways to make each other lightheaded. The love in this poem makes making love seem new again, with all the privacy and intimacy it deserves.

In 'Don't Miss Out! . . .' Imtiaz Dharker isn't shouting 'this is a poem about sex in midlife', but indeed it is. The couple in the poem are left dizzy and breathless. Away from the glare and glitz and manipulation in the *Buy this Experience! Don't Miss Out!* of the title, the poem offers a powerful and sensual thrust of its own. It's a delicious alternative to chasing experience as if time's running out.

Imtiaz Dharker is skilled in poetry, painting, and film directing. You can see her visual interests in the shapeliness of this poem – perhaps it's a sand-filled hourglass; a reminder too that time isn't eternal. As the poem's stanzas narrow there's a shedding of layers, a narrowing down, a focus. This thirty-three-line poem has only six complete sentences within it, some of them long, some very short. To read this poem aloud requires modulation of breath and lungs – in contrast to the clipped, imperative sentences of the title. Maybe the shape of the poem is the sound of breath after climax, bodies collapsing into each other. Certainly breath is a theme: dizzy altitudes and lightheadedness, thin blue air and breathlessness.

This poem is an elegy, from the ancient Greek word *elegos* meaning a song or poem of lamentation. The shape of the poem might tell of things running out, but the breath and breadth of the poem is of fulfilment, satisfaction, body and desire and connection and exploration. In Dharker's brilliant hands, the elegiac poem is one that bursts with life and spontaneity.

The word 'you' is present throughout this poem, especially in the first half: 'I look at you', 'miles / to go before I know you', 'become familiar with you', 'I seek out your shore, you stalk my / tigers', 'your / kiss', 'your mouth'. In the second stanza, the language of their lovemaking moves from *you* to *we/us*. However the *you* returns in the final sentence:

You Are
Here

The capital letters for these three words, as well as the italics, make the words stand out. *Wish you were here!* is what's imagined to be said in postcards. There's no wishing in this poem; there's pure being. Knowing that Dharker's husband had already died a few years before this poem was published, I see the three final words of this poem as a memory, as a moment of missing him, as a moment of feeling him, right in the here, right in the now. The poem's final line is just one word: *Here.* And *Here* is where the poet is, too, in the wake of her lover's sad death, with these glad memories of big plans being spontaneously interrupted by nothing more than just being with one another. The poem spins itself into a solitary word, a word of arrival, a word of presence. Solitary, yes, but not abandoned.

I've loved nature poetry all my life but never felt inclined to write it – I never felt like I had the emotional relationship with the landscape that'd make my writing any more than plain description. I grew up in the countryside, and took long walks throughout my teenage years: from our townland named after the ruined castle, to the shore where an old round fortress stood. Still, I never felt the urge to write nature poetry.

Maybe it's a stage of life, maybe it's the pandemic, maybe it's the loss of a friend who used to phone me up saying *The goldfinches have returned!* but I'm writing poems about nature now, and reading them even more.

A Blessing

James Wright

Just off the highway to Rochester, Minnesota,
Twilight bounds softly forth on the grass.
And the eyes of those two Indian ponies
Darken with kindness.
They have come gladly out of the willows
To welcome my friend and me.
We step over the barbed wire into the pasture
Where they have been grazing all day, alone.
They ripple tensely, they can hardly contain their
    happiness
That we have come.
They bow shyly as wet swans. They love each other.
There is no loneliness like theirs.
At home once more,
They begin munching the young tufts of spring in the
    darkness.
I would like to hold the slenderer one in my arms,
For she has walked over to me
And nuzzled my left hand.
She is black and white,
Her mane falls wild on her forehead,
And the light breeze moves me to caress her long ear
That is delicate as the skin over a girl's wrist.
Suddenly I realize
That if I stepped out of my body I would break
Into blossom.

When I was sixteen, my older sister Áine asked me if I'd like to hear a string quartet one evening. She'd got free tickets to see the Vanbrugh Quartet play Dvořák's String Quartet in F Major, a piece more commonly known as the *American Quartet*. I got the bus into town, made my way to the university, and sat next to her in a wood-panelled room on an uncomfortable chair. Listening to the recital, I was overwhelmed by the sound four small instruments could make together. The next day, back at school, I knew that if I tried to describe what I'd experienced I'd fail, and in that failing, something would be lost. I held the music and the memory in me like a secret.

Many people have experiences of such beauty: a sunset, a conversation with a friend or stranger, a golden moment of happiness, a birth, or even a death. It can be hard to know how to describe moments of such purity, so I understand why many choose not to. James Wright, in this most beautiful of poems, manages to gather beauty and companionship and silence and poise into one hundred and seventy-two words. Even reading these gorgeous lines of his, I'm made shy: shy about the possibility of ever describing beauty.

This poem is set at night. The images of the poem – the ponies, the willows, the fence, the poet and his friend, the 'young tufts of spring' – are all so vibrant that it's easy to imagine the poem's action happening in daylight. But

Wright is describing what he himself could barely see. It was twilight, the softness of the early night, and two friends have come '[j]ust off the highway to Rochester, Minnesota'.

It always seems to me that the two friends go to this field because they know they'll find the ponies there. 'And the eyes of those two Indian ponies . . .' he writes, and later, 'they have been grazing all day, alone'. How does he know this if he doesn't already know them? This is a return, not a surprise. This is a poem about familiarity and the needed hospitality of animals.

My dad has a friend who is a robin. The robin comes to the back door every day, which my dad leaves open. He's a great whistler – my father, not the bird – and when the small animal arrives my dad starts mimicking its song. These days the bird comes in and takes crumbs from the table. Once it hopped on the skillet and looked around the kitchen while my dad took snaps. When he works in the garden planting seeds, the robin hops alongside him, eating some of the seeds my father has just planted. Both of them animals, both whistling. The trust of an animal is a good thing; James Wright knows that, and the extraordinary reach of this poem shares his knowledge. It's like the landscape and the night are all alive with generosity. The twilight 'bounds softly' and the eyes of the ponies '[d]arken with kindness' as they come 'gladly out of the willows / To welcome my friend and me'. This is not a poem about anguish, but a poem that describes the welcomes the world hides alongside its sorrows. This is not a poem ignorant of isolation – 'There is no loneliness like theirs' – but it is a poem alive with what a drop of consolation can mean in a time of desolation. What is it like to be welcomed by those ponies with such warmth?

The ponies in 'A Blessing' are as delighted to see the friends as the friends are delighted to see them, hardly able to contain their happiness. In them, loneliness and together-ness are blended. They have been looking forward to the visit of the friends, the poem suggests, and this visit allows them to be 'At home once more'. Why are they lonely? Because they are alive. Why are they happy? Because they are alive. Are we talking about the ponies? Or are we talking about the men? We are.

James Wright, a poet and a US Army veteran from Ohio, had a difficult life. This poem appeared in a collection titled *The Branch Will Not Break*, published originally in 1963, which considers the Second World War and its impact on him. In many of the poems he is out in nature troubling what has sometimes been called human nature: death, decay, war, kindness and consolation.

The title of this poem – 'A Blessing' – is intriguing. Who is blessing whom? There are many answers to this question, I'm sure, but I can never get beyond the idea that it's the ponies who bless the men. The ponies bow, and in their tenderness, their vulnerability, their unabashed delight, the men find echoes of their own gentle natures, perhaps gentle natures they've abandoned, or denied. Wright wishes to 'hold the slenderer one in my arms'. He looks at her, at her colours, and reaches out to touch the delicate skin of her ear. She lets him. Often, a blessing is offered by a priest. Is the pony the priest in this poem? I think so. He goes to her, in the same way some people go to a minister, or an oracle, but he is not looking for absolution, or guidance, or instruction. He is looking to meet tenderness with tender-ness. The pony gives him what she is able; she brings the same out in him.

This poem is renowned for many good reasons – its setting and music and gentleness – but among poets it's often praised for its almost perfect final lines:

Suddenly I realize
That if I stepped out of my body I would break
Into blossom.

A poem's flow is often a set of contradictions: the line enjambs – is broken – for the eye, but the sentence continues without interruption. So this poem is saying that if James Wright stepped out of his body he 'would break'; and, at the same time, that if he stepped out of his body he 'would break / Into blossom.' The linebreak allows for different things to be simultaneously true, an ending and a flowering. Which one is it? I don't know; both, I suppose. It could simply be that after the ravages of war, the experience of being welcomed and nuzzled by two ponies was an almost unbearable blessing. In our own griefs it can be hard to make space for pleasure. People can destroy joy because they wish for it so much. It takes courage to welcome gladness while you're carrying something else. The speaker in this poem is able to seek joy out. He drives along the highway to a turnoff that he knows. He brings a friend. They share. They do not break, or at least not too much. Their nightmares bloom and blossom with delight. The poem holds breaking along with blossom; we wish for the same for all who've made their way through similar battles.

One of the wondrous things about poetry is that it knows a lot about constraint. If I were to be asked to tell the story of my life I wouldn't know where to start; it'd depend on the day. But a poem knows that I don't need to tell *the* story of my life, rather, I can just tell *a* story. A single experience can sometimes contain worlds of meaning.

The Word

Zaffar Kunial

I couldn't tell you now what possessed me
to shut summer out and stay in my room.
Or at least attempt to. In bed mostly.
It's my dad, standing in the door frame
not entering – but pausing to shape advice
that keeps coming back. 'Whatever is matter,

must *enjoy the life*.' He pronounced this twice.
And me, I heard wrongness in putting a *the*

before *life*. In two minds. Ashamed. Aware.
That I knew better, though was stuck inside
while the sun was out. That I'm native here.
In a halfway house. Like that sticking word.
That definite article, half right, half
wrong, still present between *enjoy* and *life*.

So much of what's called *lyric poetry* is a reflection on the 'I'. Lyric poetry is so called because of an old practice where Greek poets strummed the lyre – a small, harp-like instrument – while they recited their poems. I don't know anyone who does that anymore (although I do know someone who recites filthy nursery rhymes while accompanying herself on the cello), but the term has stuck. Lyric poems have a certain musicality to them, and are also often poems in which the poet speaks in the first person.

To have a poem that speaks from the 'I' might make us think that this 'I' will present itself confidently: *I am the Poet and therefore I am describing my known self when I write this poem about Me*. But this brilliant short poem by Zaffar Kunial starts off with an admission that even the person speaking about themselves doesn't understand themselves. 'I couldn't tell you now what possessed me / to shut summer out and stay in my room'.

When I read this poem, I'm instantly brought back to my teenage years, when Moods had capital letters, when phrases like 'I Hate Everything' were my defence against the Everything. Zaffar shut himself in his room as a teenager; I went on ten-mile walks – not for health, just to get away. This poem is written from the vantage point of an adult who doesn't understand the teenager he was, so what hope did the poet's dad have? The young man has shut his door on life and parents and care and friends and summer. He's in bed. Is he depressed, or is he fifteen? Maybe both.

'Whatever is matter, // must *enjoy the life*' are the father's offending words. Perhaps nothing is the matter. Perhaps it's just the burden of self-consciousness piling on top of a teenager. Perhaps he's so filled with desire and possibility that he shuts them out by keeping windows and curtains and doors closed. Perhaps he wants to enjoy his life, but doesn't yet know how to enjoy enjoying it. Maybe he feels alone. Maybe he fears feeling alone. Reading this poem now, I connect with this poem's expression of anger, lethargy, exhaustion, denial and possibility; the stuff of all age, not just youth. Teenagers, perhaps, just feel some of life's complexities in a particularly intense way.

The poet's dad is 'standing in the door frame / not entering'. Why wouldn't he enter? Perhaps he has an intuitive understanding of not trespassing; perhaps he's as bewildered about what's going on as the son is. He offers mild advice: '*enjoy the life.*' Isn't advice one of the hardest things to ask for, and one of the hardest things to take? I find myself wondering how long the father in this poem stood outside the door wondering what to say.

There's distance between the young man and the father. They're father and son, of course, which is a certain bond and a certain gulf. One is in bed on a summer's day and the other is standing at an open door facing into a room that's trying to shut out the sun. But there's another gulf, perhaps the one that's most powerful: language – and, underneath language, shame. Zaffar Kunial's mother was English, and his father is from Kashmir; his father speaks a dialect of Punjabi as well as Urdu, and here, in the father's words of advice, we hear what might technically be called grammatical mistakes.

'Whatever is matter, // must *enjoy the life*.' Perhaps some grammarians would correct the father's sentence to 'Whatever is the matter, you must enjoy life' or 'Whatever's the matter with you, you must enjoy life'. What's clear is that the space between the fluent British-born son and his second-language father is causing the differences of pluri-cultured families to expand. Here, the father is speaking in the language his son uses, urging him outside, into the sun.

'I heard wrongness in putting a *the* // before *life*.' What is the shame in this poem? That his father doesn't speak dictionary-perfect English? Is the speaker ashamed of himself for being ashamed of that? Is he ashamed of himself for being stuck in this awkward phase of teenagerhood, or for having a dad who stands at the door, giving good advice he can't accept? Is he ashamed of being seen? This is the unbridgeable gap between the speaker *now* – the poet who can write in perfect sentences – and the speaker as a young man, filled with shame at things that weren't shameful.

It's useful to return to the title of the poem: 'The Word'. At first glance, I find myself wondering *what word?* But the answer is there already: the definite article, the word '*the*' – a coding that maps the cultural and linguistic distance between father and son. This isn't a poem about having an inadequate father; in fact, he's full of courtesy, and perhaps desperation. He's called 'my dad' rather than a more formal-sounding 'my father'. The young man in the poem is in a halfway house – of language, adulthood, culture and identity.

I think about the furies I contained as a teenager. Freud said that part of the role of being a teenager is to make your parents hate you enough that they'll be able to cope when you move away. I think I had to learn to hate myself enough, too, to grow up. Anger was its own intelligence, but I had to learn to listen, to turn away from turning it on others or myself. All this took time.

One of the glorious things this poem does is praise the vernacular use of English. When I was younger, my mother always asked *Are your homework done?* I remember feeling annoyed at the *are*, and hoping that none of my friends would ever overhear it. Towards the end of 'The Word' Kunial doesn't just highlight incomprehensible teenage angst and then pass it off; he turns, with integrity, to the words of his father. The 'the' is the 'sticking word'– 'half right, half / wrong'. He's still thinking about 'enjoy the life' and instead of seeing it as a grammatical error, he's entertaining the possibility that the error was his. 'Enjoy the life' that you *have* rather than the life you pine for, perhaps. 'Enjoy the life' that I'm giving you. Time is a force in this poem because the poem is narrated by a grown-up remembering his younger self. Older now, he reflects – perhaps with the same confusion his own father had – on everything that held him down during sunny days, leaving us to wonder what eventually helped him change.

I used to think that nature poetry was only about nature: trees, or ponies, or the way the sunlight falls on the water. My recognition of what *nature* is didn't include people. I was wrong. We humans are part of the natural world – desires and death and dominance and domesticity – and as such, it's a good thing to consider the human animal alongside other animals in poems that explore nature.

Bullshit

Vahni (Anthony) Capildeo

How to 'lose' or 'abandon' a word? Put it in jail, throw away the key? Then in every reference book or text block, an opaque rectangle shining where it used to be; a myriad lids to a single oubliette. A fort cut out of yellow, living rock; the particular sightlessness that, with the tide, saturates the underground chamber. This is 'having a concrete imagination'. Not breezeblocks. Wet stuff, instantly; ready to be footprinted.

'Bullshit' is the word I would ease into pasture. One year in an élite institution, my progressive male colleagues kept saying 'Bullshit!' They would get me alone; lean in; ask the really-really-really questions. A little way into my her-answers, they would roar in my face: 'Bullshit!' Eyes pared, jaws gaping, a warlock pack of Jacks of Clubs.

If I seemed quiet, it was because of what I was seeing.

Near my childhood home in a new city, a bull is being led down from the low hills. He walks through the diplomatic area to an empty lot. His haunches a big black valentine, swaying. He dumps as he goes. The asphalt doubly steaming.

A great bull is shitting on my street. Let him have quiet enjoyment.

What is a word you would retire from English if you could? My mother despises the word *actually* and we were forbidden to say it when we were younger. She thought that children who said *actually* sounded like children who thought they were important, and the Ireland I grew up in was clear on this: children are not important. I mentioned this forbidding of the *A*-word to her a few years ago and she said she still agreed with herself: *actually* should actually be forbidden.

People have many reasons for disliking a particular word: they do not like the sound; it's offensive or derogatory; it's inaccurate; they have a memory of someone who overused the word, or pronounced it in a particular way (my biology teacher always pronounced *capsule* as *kap-shool* and I rarely use the word to this day). Perhaps the word is associated with a particular period of your life you wish to close the door on; perhaps the word's suggestive or insipid or contains threat. Say any word often enough and it's likely to turn peculiar: word, word, word, wrrrd, wrd, whurrd, whorrde.

Vahni (Anthony) Capildeo's prose poem 'Bullshit' turns its attention to the singular word of its title. The objection to the word is not because of how it sounds, however, but because of an extended period of time at an 'élite institution' – a university – when it was used by 'progressive male colleagues'. Presumably in the men's imagination they considered themselves progressive, therefore they couldn't be considered misogynists. But the poem knows differently, explaining the men's habits of getting Vahni alone before asking questions, then repeatedly questioning the responses to those questions: 'really- / really-really'. In the eyes of these men, Vahni does not give answers, rather 'her-answers' – a forceful gendering intended, perhaps, to demean the intellectual capacity of anyone not considered male; or categorise female answers as defensive, or evasive without taking male tactics into consideration. The men roar 'Bullshit!'. It seems their roar was their aim all along.

Vahni (Anthony) Capildeo – who uses they/them pronouns – offers this extraordinary line, set apart from the stanzas on either side:

If I seemed quiet, it was because of what I was seeing.

What is the speaker of this poem seeing? They are seeing men in an élite environment shouting 'Bullshit!'; men who, perhaps, know little about actual shit from actual bulls. Despite the fact that they're entitled discerners of truth, there is a gap between what these men say and what they know.

'Eyes pared, jaws gaping . . .' the men operate as a pack. The 'Jacks of Clubs' could mean so much: a winning card; a game; a competition; an entertainer; an educator; a charming lover, given to deceit. The men in this poem do not doubt themselves, even though Capildeo draws a distinction between what they say and what they know. Do the men know how they're perceived? Would they care? Their eyes and jaws and pack mentality tell a story their words would deny: they are interested in winning, not learning. They're on the hunt, roaring like animals, but they resist any knowledge that would challenge their own behaviour.

A prose poem is an exercise in contradiction: prose and poetry are incompatible in some people's minds, so a prose poem is the arranging of unexpected pairs. The men delight in shouting out a word they have not witnessed. But the speaker of this poem uses 'concrete imagination' to pair the abstract with the actual. The poem's landscape changes and we see a bull being led down from a hill and taking a shit on the street. The bull 'walks through the diplomatic area' to the empty lot and defecates as he goes, with no regard for diplomacy or property. On the one hand what's being described is as natural as anything: a bull doesn't care for toilet etiquette. Rather than push back against the word 'bullshit' Capildeo offers an argument for it: it is everywhere – if the men think élite institutions are devoid of shit, then they are not paying attention.

For the past few years, I've lived next to a field. In the mornings I see foxes and hares in the field. Cows meander down midmorning and stay till night. One evening I was standing at the fence looking at the cows when I saw the bull approaching. I'd never seen him before and I laughed out loud. He reminded me of some men I've known, all swagger and stage; walking so as to pivot their muscle round their sex. Is the bull in the poem – the maker of the bullshit – being praised for its animal nature? Certainly, Capildeo wishes this bull its own quiet and its own contentment. Perhaps Capildeo is saying *let animals be animals.*

And yet there's a question in this poem about why these men, in this place, feel able to call 'Bullshit!' wherever they see fit. The men and the bull feel at home, shitting where they please. However, the bull isn't its own master: it's led. What leads those men? There's a question at the heart of the poem about how a place can shape behaviour, and

Capildeo is questioning the place and powers that shape the behaviours of these 'progressive' men.

It's easy to forget the opening line of this poem: 'How to "lose" or "abandon" a word?' Capildeo imagines an emptiness in every dictionary where a lost word would have been, each empty space where that word would have been looking like a lid to an oubliette – a secret dungeon accessed only by an overhead door, coming from the French word for 'forget'. The opening stanza also troubles the word 'concrete', recognising that it, too, comes in different forms: breezeblocks, yes; but also wet, able to carry the shape of a hand or foot pressed into it. Under all of this, I hear a question about whether the nature of a thing can change. Even concrete was malleable once. Can a bull be led? Clearly. Can these men? That's unclear. A prose poem is a perfect form for this complicated question, combining two seemingly contradictory things in justified blocks of text. If a poem can be reshaped, if concrete can be poured, if even a bull can be guided, what about so-called élite and progressive men?

Every now and then Paul, my partner, will say 'I like you' to me. We've always been an affectionate couple, but those moments when he says *like* have a lovely quality to them. Maybe it's just me, but somehow *I like you* can feel more casual – but also more intentional – than *love.*

Some Things I Like

Lemn Sissay

(*A poem to shout*)

I like wrecks, I like ex-junkies,
I like flunks and ex-flunkies,
I like the way the career-less career,
I like flat beer,
I like people who tell half stories and forget the rest,
I like people who make doodles in important written tests,
I like being late. I like fate. I like the way teeth grate,
I like laceless shoes cordless blues,
I like the one-bar blues,
I like buttonless coats and leaky boats,
I like rubbish tips and bitten lips,
I like yesterday's toast,
I like cold tea, I like reality,
I like ashtrays, I write and like crap plays.

I like curtains that don't quite shut,
I like bread knives that don't quite cut,
I like rips in blue jeans,
I like people who can't say what they mean,
I like spiders with no legs, pencils with no lead,
Ants with no heads, worms that are half dead.
I like holes, I like coffee cold. I like creases in neat folds.
I like signs that just don't know where they're going,
I like angry poems,
I like the way you can't pin down the sea.
See.

Lemn Sissay's attention towards the word *like* in 'Some Things I Like' feels casual, everyday, easily done, but also deliberate, considered and spacious. It's an open door, and as such, a place of hospitality. It's easy to say, and in this way, can be radical. I saw him perform at a festival a few years ago. His recital was electrifying, uplifting and connecting. How can a person address a crowd of a thousand and make you feel like you've been returned to yourself while also being expanded? I don't know how, but I know the answer: it's Lemn Sissay.

The poem has a rhythm, a percussion of sound: thirty repeated likes: everything from flat beer to wrecks, buttonless coats, yesterday's toast and angry poems. Lemn likes people (especially people who've been discarded); he likes leisure, he likes things that other people reject; he likes it when a person forgets where they are in a story. The seeming nonchalance of these lists is anything but random: he likes things that don't quite hold together, things that don't open properly, things that don't close. 'I like reality' he says. There's that word again: *like*, from the Old English *līcian,* meaning 'to be found pleasing'.

The more I think about this poem, the more I consider it to be a poem of attention to displacement. I am drawn to the objects he mentions – 'rubbish tips and bitten lips' – I'm drawn to the verb 'like'; and perhaps, to go a little deeper again, I'm drawn to the 'I'. It's the capacity of the speaker in this poem to look around, and see, and create connection where disconnection has been assumed that moves me, over and over.

Lemn Sissay is a renowned British poet. He was placed in the care system at two months old, and his mother's wishes to have him back in her custody when she was better able to care for him were ignored. He was given the name of his social worker, Norman, and fostered by a family who, when he was twelve, returned him to the care system saying the devil had got into him. The rest of his youth was spent going from care home to care home, from one abusive situation to another. Even at the age of eighteen, when he was released from the system into accommodation without even a bed, he wasn't given all the information he asked for. All he was given was an old letter from his mother begging for his return, and a document detailing his original name: Lemn Sissay (Lemn meaning *why* in Amharic, the language his Ethiopian mother spoke). Since then, he's campaigned on behalf of young people in care; fought the care system for compensation; and raised his voice about institutional and embedded racism in a system that should be providing shelter from abuse not opportunities for it. He's lauded in poetry and in public life, and has received awards, honorary doctorates and respect. It is a brutal background to have survived. He is a brilliant poet. The private details of his life are a demonstration of how public policy can fail utterly. He shares this; it takes a toll. He carries scars. He is magnificent. All of these things are true.

The heart of this poem is generosity. It carries an intuitive understanding of people who've felt left out, embarrassed, ashamed, undone, uninvited, unpolished at telling stories, worried their inadequacies will be found out. *It's okay*, the poem says, *I like it.* Lemn makes art from things that don't fit in, rhyming 'ex-junkies' with 'ex-flunkies', 'ashtrays' with 'crap plays', and 'blue jeans' with 'people who can't say what they mean'. I don't know Lemn Sissay, but when I read this poem I imagine he's talking to anyone who is surviving a lifetime of rejection – whether they're fourteen or fifty – telling them that their quirks, their habits, the forgotten corners they go to in order to feel okay, are all okay. He gathers experiences of rejection and puts them in a poem that builds its own velocity of liking and acceptance. In this way, the form of the poem is a visual and audible manifestation of the poem's impulses: celebration, momentum, energy, life. The voice in this poem is one of kindness, a voice that says art can be made here too. *Beauty is in the eye of the beholder,* we say, and I think *liking* is too. It's Lemn's looking that makes things likeable.

In a poem about quirky likes, it's not just quirks that get attention, it's wrecks too: it's the career-less, the people who doodle on tests, who are late, who don't have the clothes to dress to impress, who feel inadequate. There are headless ants, half-dead worms, and spiders with no legs in this poem. Who's doing that to the ants and worms? The poem is trying to make a landscape where rage is understood. 'I like angry poems' he writes towards the end of a poem whose instructive epigraph is '*A poem to shout*'. Rage informs this piece of art. This poem knows the inside of rejection, and from that same inside, writes welcome. There's no self-pity in the poem, and there's no categorisation either: 'I like the way you can't pin down the sea' he says, writing about something vast and changing; something that draws the eye, but is uncontainable; something of power and consolation; something that moves in and moves out. The poem finishes with a single-word sentence: 'See.' It's not a question; it's not *See?* It's an imperative, an instruction, an order. Who's he telling to see? Me, I think, and anyone like me who doesn't see what – and who, and how – Lemn Sissay sees.

I have a name that is frequently mispronounced, so if someone is unfamiliar with how to say it, I'm not bothered. But I've been in situations where a person deliberately mispronounces my name, anglicising it to Patrick, refusing any attempt to pronounce it properly.

It's an old wound, that trick: the Irish language was suppressed by policy and practice for centuries. How a person's name is pronounced – or mispronounced – carries power. Reading poetry from around the world, I come across so many poets who write about their name: the story behind it, the reason they like it pronounced properly, the history it evokes when someone won't even try.

Say My Name
Meleika Gesa-Fatafehi

Thank you Dad, for my name.
Thank you Mum, for letting me keep it.
Thank you Sydney Nan, for saying my name lovingly every time.
Lastly, thank you Papa and Nan, and the rest of my ancestors,
I dedicate this all to you.

My name was my name before
                I walked among the living
     before I could breathe
     before I had lungs to fill
before my great grandmother passed
     and everyone was left to grieve

My name was birthed from a dream
     a whisper from gods to a king
     a shout into the stars that produced
           another that shone as bright
They held me without being burnt, humming lullabies in pidgin

My name was passed down from my
     ancestors
They acknowledged my roots grew in two
     places
So, they ripped my name from the ocean
     and mixed it into the bloodlines of my totems

My name has survived the destruction of worlds
And the genocidal rebirthing of so-called ones

It's escaped the overwhelmed jaw of the death bringer
  many a time
It has survived the conflicts that resulted in my gods,
  from both lands, knowing me as kin,
But noticing that I am painfully unrecognisable and lost
They are incapable of understanding
  the foreign tongue that was forced on me

My name has escaped cyclones and their daughters
It has been blessed by the dead
As they mixed dirt, salt and liquid red,
  into my flesh
My name is the definition of resilience
It is a warrior that manifested because of warriors

So, excuse me as I roll my eyes or sigh as you
Mispronounce my name
  over and over again
Or when you give me another
  that dishonours my mothers and fathers
That doesn't acknowledge my lineage to my island home
Or the scents of rainforest and ocean foam
You will not stand here on stolen land
  and whitewash my name
For it is two words intertwined
  holding as much power as a hurricane
Say it right or don't say it at all
For I am Meleika
  I will answer when you call

Meleika Gesa-Fatafehi (they/them) is a Torres Strait Islander and Tongan poet and storyteller who lives in what is now called Australia. 'Say My Name' explores the importance of naming. It asserts, with strength, validity, truth and power – the power of a hurricane – that a name should be known, then pronounced correctly and not made to sound like something else. Association, while it can be a helpful memorisation device, is exposed as laziness, or suppression. This poem knows that a name carries within it heritage, story, dignity and resistance to empire and colonisation.

Meleika Gesa-Fatafehi's name is a living reminder of lineages and places that should always have remained independent. The poem's sense of power comes from its deep intuition of the dignity of self-narration – a self-narration that has been undermined by the European projects for so long. Lyric poetry finds an echo in Meleika's poem: the Indigenous 'I' challenges the long legacies of European colonialism in the Pacific, and the limitation of a European imagination of 'I' is exposed for how it luxuriated in what it gave to itself, all the while destroying nations and their peoples. In the economy of this poem, to shape a sentence that uses first-person pronouns (I, me, we) is a political act: speaking clearly to powers that sought to destroy them.

While 'Say My Name' focuses on a particularity of place, it also opens up a temporal, and even liminal, sense of space and time. 'My name was my name before / I walked among the living / before I could breathe [. . .] birthed from a dream / a whisper from gods to a king'. Who is speaking here? Some god, both young and old? Yes.

There's a quest, a task, a level of rising to the dignity of being called to be a representative in conversation with the past. Gesa-Fatafehi is representing the mothers and the fathers that have come before, the people to whom the poem is dedicated, and the people who carry languages in their memory, even languages that have been taken away. At times the poem is a challenge to people who'd assume forgiveness for lazy mispronunciations of Meleika Gesa-Fatafehi. But at other times the poem itself is a conversation with ancestors. To both, the final line rings true, but with utterly different inferences: 'I will answer when you call' – I will answer when you summon me, or I will answer when you take the time to pronounce my name correctly.

The energy of this poem is directed to assertion and affirmation: assertion against the demeaning forces of colonisation; affirmation of the dignity of lineage. 'Say My Name' recognises that when an Indigenous language has been destroyed, a permanent lament is established amongst the populations who spoke that language, and the populations who come after: 'noticing that I am painfully unrecognisable and lost / They are incapable of understanding / the foreign tongue that was forced on me'. Here, the old gods don't understand Meleika. People – together with their ancestors and gods – are linguistically displaced. However, even in the reality of this linguistic gulf between the speaker and their gods, the story of Meleika Gesa-Fatafehi's name is affirmed like a creation narrative. Their name was 'birthed from a dream' and whispered from 'gods to a king' before being shouted into the universe, the shout itself creating a star that could be held 'without being burnt'.

Ancestors shared stories in their own language over this newborn. While understanding has been denied, language is still its own power, and the memory of it having been spoken is not completely undone, even if understanding has been. The poem is at once an argument for epistemology – it is possible to learn how to pronounce someone's name correctly – as well as an argument for the kind of connection that transcends comprehension.

The final stanza opens with 'So, excuse me as I roll my eyes or sigh as you / Mispronounce my name / over and over again'. Mispronunciation isn't a one-off experience: the 'over and over again' demonstrates how – for someone whose language, land and culture have been oppressed – being misnamed echoes backwards and forwards in time.

Among the many people who are thanked in the opening dedication of the poem are 'Dad, for my name' and 'Mum, for letting me keep it'. With them is 'Sydney Nan, for saying my name lovingly every time'. This, then, is an intergenerational endeavour: naming; permission to keep a name that others would erase; the necessity of a name being pronounced with love. A dedication like this is both personal and political. When, later in the poem, Meleika states that forcing another name on them dishonours their 'mothers and fathers' it is a family line that's dishonoured, not just an individual. 'I contain multitudes' we hear in a poem by Walt Whitman. This poem asserts the same: multiple origins, energies living in the poet, seas and bloodlines and roots and time and air. This elemental poem amplifies the connection between language and location, linking the past and the present through yearning and assertion.

There are entire sections of my family tree that are lost due to the famine in Ireland. One great-great grandfather was left alone, at the age of seven, and brought up by a kindly schoolteacher. I've always assumed his brother and parents and other family members died and are buried in a mass grave somewhere in West Cork, but my mother wonders whether any of them made it onto a boat bound for America. If they did get there, where did they land, and where did they go? What did they do for work? More importantly, what kind of neighbours were they?

Miscegenation

Natasha Trethewey

In 1965 my parents broke two laws of Mississippi;
they went to Ohio to marry, returned to Mississippi.

They crossed the river into Cincinnati, a city whose name
begins with a sound like *sin*, the sound of wrong – *mis* in Mississippi.

A year later they moved to Canada, followed a route the same
as slaves, the train slicing the white glaze of winter, leaving Mississippi.

Faulkner's Joe Christmas was born in winter, like Jesus, given his name
for the day he was left at the orphanage, his race unknown in Mississippi.

My father was reading *War and Peace* when he gave me my name.
I was born near Easter, 1966, in Mississippi.

When I turned 33 my father said, *It's your Jesus year – you're the same
age he was when he died*. It was spring, the hills green in Mississippi.

I know more than Joe Christmas did. Natasha is a Russian name –
though I'm not; it means *Christmas child*, even in Mississippi.

From the first line, it's clear this history-laden poem 'Miscegenation' will address laws that banned interracial marriage in the United States. A change in federal law overthrew such prohibitions in 1967, but some individual states took years to overturn them in their state constitutions. In Mississippi, not only was miscegenation illegal, but interracial couples who married in other states were not permitted to return to their state.

Alongside these laws, Natasha Trethewey's poem also references the northward migration of enslaved Black American people; a novel by Faulkner; Russian literature; the gospels; the marriage of the poet's parents; and the story and meaning behind her first name. If you were to set a writing prompt something like: *Combine Mississippi's anti-miscegenation laws, with references to your family, cities, time, religion, transportation, and the years 1965 and '66 in a poem of no more than 170 words*, a class might say that such a thing was impossible. But Natasha Trethewey has combined all of these threads in a poem whose elegance is aided, not interrupted, by its many references.

Knowing how to say multiple things in a short space of time is a rich art, and this art is helped by the employment of a poetic form. A form is a shape on the page, but also a kind of music. This poem's form is a ghazal. Ghazals are written in couplets; from five up to fifteen. Sometimes a poem unfolds only one idea, but a ghazal holds many different ideas together. This is achieved by the repetition of a word at the end of every couplet – in this case, *Mississippi*. The ghazal is originally an Arabic form; ghazal is the way the word *gazelle* gets into English: an animal with speed and elegance, and that can change direction quickly. A ghazal poem can, too – the couplets go in many different directions, but the repeated word holds all the lines together.

Natasha Trethewey had a white father and a Black mother, and she's written widely about how she was treated differently depending on where she was, or which parent she was with. If she was out with her father, she might be perceived as passing for white; if she was out with her mother, she might be treated better than her mother, because she was perceived as 'less Black' than her parent. Writing about this poem, Natasha Trethewey shared that for years she'd had unrelated ideas, like threads: the story of her name; the story of place; the story of the laws that affected her family, but she was unsure how to hold them together. When she realized a ghazal has couplets, but the couplets don't have to follow directly on from each other – that it can spin different threads together with a repeated word – she understood that this was the form that could hold disparate experiences of her personal and political existence in shape. Through the repeated word in this poem – Mississippi – she holds beautiful and brutal things together: marriages and laws; departures and names; novels and history. Mississippi, Mississippi, Mississippi.

'Miscegenation' looks at the experience of an individual life and traces that life through law, literature, history and society. It asks its readers to reflect on the laws and circumstances central to their families' story. Place-names in this poem carry coded warnings: Cincinnati for instance, a word whose first syllable could also be read as 'sin'. Whose sin? The sin of the white world that wrote and upheld miscegenation laws? By taking apart the name of that city, Trethewey is inviting a certain moral examination of where sin *really* lies. Behind the story of a place is the story of the laws within that place, and that place will be narrated differently depending on your experience of power; *sin* in Cincinnati; *mis* in Mississippi. The repeated word functions as a way of holding something to the light, seeing what it contains, both the wicked and the good. I read this poem and think of Irish migration to Mississippi, wondering which Irish names were signatories to those terrible laws.

Mississippi isn't the only music in 'Miscegenation'. In addition to the repetition, the poem states 'I know more than Joe Christmas did', reminiscent of Nina Simone's 1964 song 'Mississippi Goddam' with its refrain of 'everybody knows'. Nina Simone sang that song in front of ten thousand people on the Selma to Montgomery marches. The song was banned in many southern states; records that had been distributed to radio stations were sometimes returned to the distributor snapped in half. With this deft reference to *knowing* Natasha Trethewey has brought Nina Simone's brilliance into conversation with the long tradition of ghazal.

In formal ghazal poems, the poet always makes a reference – direct or obscure – to their own name, like a signature. Natasha does this brilliantly in that same line with her reference to Joe Christmas (from William Faulkner's novel *Light in August*), a character who doesn't know his origins and believes himself to be of mixed-race heritage. He'd been named for the day he was found, Christmas Day. Natasha

Trethewey – whose first name means Christmas in Russian – was given her name by her father, who was reading Tolstoy at Easter in 1966. Unlike Joe Christmas, she knows where she comes from, and in 'Mississippi' she holds much together.

A few years ago, Boris Johnson, who was the Foreign Secretary of the British government at the time, later Prime Minister, began reciting the Rudyard Kipling poem 'Mandalay' while he was waiting for proceedings to begin during a formal reception in Myanmar. It was all caught on camera, as was the speedy hushing that came from a British diplomat. 'Not appropriate,' the diplomat said, through clenched lips.

A poem is not just a poem, it's a way of looking at the world; and that particular poem of Kipling's is rife with colonialism, white supremacy and entitlement. Even to a fellow British government employee, Johnson's recitation of the poem inside the Shwedagon Pagoda – a sacred site – was not taken as a bit of bluff or whimsy. Rather, it was interpreted as a statement validating the British Empire's violent occupation of Myanmar from 1824-1948. 'Not appropriate' indeed.

Reporting Back to Queen Isabella
Lorna Goodison

When Don Cristobal returned to a hero's welcome,
his caravels corked with treasures of the New World,
he presented his findings; told of his great adventures
to Queen Isabella, whose speech set the gold standard
for her nation's language. When he came to Xamaica
he described it so: 'The fairest isle that eyes ever beheld.'
Then he balled up a big sheet of parchment, unclenched,
and let it fall off a flat surface before it landed at her feet.
There we were, massifs, high mountain ranges, expansive
plains, deep valleys, one he'd christened for the Queen
of Spain. Overabundance of wood, over one hundred
rivers, food, and fat pastures for Spanish horses, men,
and cattle; and yes, your majesty, there were some people.

For the last few years, I've read all the works of one given poet over the course of twelve months. Sometimes these are living poets, other times not. It started with Emily Dickinson (she took two years), then R. S. Thomas, and then, in 2019, I moved on to Lorna Goodison, a Jamaican poet who'd initially trained as a painter. Poetry was a calling in her, though, and she says that as long as she avoided writing it, something was boiling up inside her. Toward the end of 2019, I was invited to write a profile for *Image* journal and was thrilled to have the opportunity to speak to her after a year of immersing myself in her work. Of all her poems, 'Reporting Back to Queen Isabella' is the one I kept on returning to; for its artistry, its audacity, and for the profound control that leads the reader towards those final four words.

The poem's title introduces the pageantry and theatre. Someone is reporting *back* to this Queen. Who is she? She was Queen Isabella of Spain, married to Ferdinand. It was she who'd funded the travels of Christopher Columbus, named Cristobal Colón, or Don Cristobal, in Spanish. In choosing to say Don Cristobal instead of Christopher Columbus, Lorna Goodison brings the reader into an imperial Spanish sensibility. We are situated in the court of the Queen, with much pomp and ceremony that is intended to mask malice and murder and war-making.

In 1494 Christopher Columbus landed on Jamaica, an island already inhabited by the Taino, the Indigenous people of the Caribbean and Florida. The name Xamaica (spelled with an X not a J) is a Taino word, perhaps meaning 'land of wood and water' (I've also seen it rendered as 'great spirit of land of man'). The trip was a scouting trip, and now, returned, Don Cristobal stands before his royal Spanish patron a hero, with treasures and reports of the so-called New World.

Social media and contemporary economics are sometimes blamed for a weaponisation of language, but the technology of spin has been around for centuries: words like *hero* and *exploration* mask the reality of conquest and occupation. Likewise the *New World*. That New World wasn't new. These territories were sophisticated, with languages, trade arrangements, governance, spirituality, tensions, disasters, greed, joy and life. But naming it 'New' gave license to Europeans to conduct war but not call it war, to enact murder and enslavement but not call it murder and enslavement, and to corral people into European systems of belief, governance and trade at the expense of locally established systems. Language is at the start and the heart of all of this.

'Tír gan teanga, tír gan anam', we say in Irish: a land without a language is a land without a soul. That's not just a lament, it's also an accusation. To kill the soul of a people you start by killing their language. And as a result of this act of war the colonised must then adopt a new tongue in order to engage in any kind of negotiation; those are old technologies of terror.

So the 'hero' Don Cristobal presents his 'findings' of 'treasures' from the 'New World' to the Queen. The scene is theatrical: he balls up a parchment and lets it roll off the flat surface of the table. This is all happening during the childhood of Magellan, the Portuguese man who was the first to circumnavigate the world, notably also funded by the Spanish

Crown. The parchment falling off the edge of the table might imply a flat earth, or the edge of the world, or the act of laying everything at the feet of the Queen as if she's above it. Whatever the meaning, a parchment showing a map of Xamaica is at her feet.

Then a change, a little hint of rebellion. Up until now, the poem has been narrated by a neutral observer. But suddenly a speaker announces themselves: 'There we were'. The introduction of the word 'we' is vital: such a small word, and yet it inserts the identity of whosever voice we are hearing, a voice that is watching empire congratulate itself while asserting an identity older than itself. A list emerges:

> massifs, high mountain ranges, expansive
> plains, deep valleys, one he'd christened for the Queen
> of Spain. Overabundance of wood, over one hundred
> rivers, and food, and fat pastures for Spanish horses, men,
> and cattle . . .

Who is speaking? The land? The people to be conquered? The people whose labour will be exploited for the profit of the few?

The lush descriptions in the list do not just describe beauty. They describe something that has been looked upon with greed, and with the entitled assumption of appropriative ownership. By shaping this long list, Goodison highlights the ways that administration, too, can be a tool of injustice. Someone had to count and map and check all those resources being totalled up for the pleasure of the Queen. How do the colonisers imagine they'll take possession of these resources? Easy: murder; weapons; enslavement; displacement; divide and conquer.

While this poem is formed by historical facts, it isn't only about history-telling. Rather than an exhaustive list of names, places, dates, reports and sequences, historical poetry narrates veritable data but places it under the power of a poetic voice. There's a theory in conflict resolution that conflicts take as long to deescalate as they took to escalate. I think anybody from a colonised or previously colonised country knows this. Oppression doesn't end the day oppressors leave; the impact of centuries can take centuries to repair. Publishing this poem in 2013, Lorna Goodison not only imagined a historical scene, but also employed a poetics of time to describe the beginnings of systems that continue, even now.

The 'we' at the beginning of the list serves as a little wink, an assertion of a voice of protest, but this doesn't end with the 'we'. The first item on the list is the word 'massif', a magnificent word choice, because depending on where you're from and who you are, you'll hear this word differently. 'Massif' is a word that people in Jamaica (and in many parts of the African diaspora) use to refer to 'a group of people'. So what seems like a list of geographical observations – 'massifs, high mountain ranges, expansive / plains, deep valleys', woods, rivers, food, and pastures – is an insertion of personhood, resistance and accountability.

The final words of the short poem – 'and yes, your majesty, there were some people' – act like a punch. Queen Isabella is reputed to have felt uncomfortable at her empire's practice of enslavement, but not to the extent that she halted it. However, the brilliance of Lorna Goodison's poem is that a voice of resistance has already asserted itself: the 'massifs' among the massifs, the 'we' speaking about themselves; there already.

When I was young, I wrote poems in a small book and carried it with me everywhere. I told almost nobody about these poems – they were full of anger and resistance, overflowing with the vulnerabilities that are contained within teenaged fury.

When I moved away from Ireland in my twenties, I gave a sealed box of these poems to a friend to keep in his attic. Years went by and we lost touch. I found out that he'd moved and the house was demolished, making way for a block of flats on the northside of Dublin. Somewhere, under the surface of other people's homes, is a small poetry-filled box of anger, threatening the foundations of the buildings.

When You Say 'Protestors' Instead of Protectors

No'u Revilla

I would call it a trick, if it wasn't so terrifying,
the way your mouth doesn't move when you
speak. Your smile, shiny as a church, but what
kind of prayer could ever be trusted without
evidence of a free tongue? On the rare occasion
sound shakes loose, words, no matter how
unmuzzled, words still go to die. In your mouth,
even womb is wound. Sometimes I dream of
tearing your throat wide open and finding there,
where stories should be born, only bleeding
bleedingbleeding. The wish to desecrate. We are,
yet again, portrayed by you, ~~the girl the Native
the water~~ the mountain who was 'asking for it.'
Your lips so Sunday still. Sometimes I almost
believe you. So it's best I keep hiding knives in
my hair, the way my grandmother – not god –
the way my grandmother intended.

This short punch of a poem is seventeen lines long. It looks like a paragraph in a newspaper, or a text lifted from the Bible. The poem's justified lines assert and protect its own borders. It is a poem that's sure of itself and is addressed to a *you*.

You is a fascinating word. In poetry, it's called the *lyric address,* meaning that poems that use the *you* are speaking to – addressing – someone. Who is the someone being spoken to? It depends on the poem. *You* may be living or dead. *You* in a poem might be a god, or a beloved pet, or the poet speaking to themselves. *You* might never have lived. *You* might be loved or hated, invented or real. *You* might be invited to speak back, or forbidden from doing so.

This poem is a corrective. No wonder it's in the shape it is: squared up – almost literally – and facing outwards, addressing a *you* that has been both powerful and abusive; a *you* that is summoned to listen. What can be understood about the *you*? The evidence is all there: their mouth doesn't move when they speak; they have a shiny smile; words of nurture are rendered violent in their mouth; they justify violence by victim-blaming; then back to those 'Sunday still' lips. There is no love lost between No'u Revilla and whomever she speaks to. Is it one person? Is she speaking to a force, a power, a trend, a population, a privilege? Is this *you* a force with many bodies?

The first line deliberates over what to do in response to misnaming: 'I would call it a trick, if it wasn't so terrifying'.

This isn't the easy accusation of a protector against an opponent, this is a voice speaking back to power where power is untrusted, unmuzzled, destructive, desecrating, eradicating, blaming. And charming, too: 'Sometimes I almost / believe you.'

If poems addressed to *you* are poems of *lyric address*, then where's the damned music, the echo of the lyre? The music of this poem has multiple layers: it has been as menacing, threatening and as poisonous as it is sweet. There is resistance in the poem, resistance that wishes to be defined as *protecting,* not just as *protesting*, so perhaps the music is in the self-definition, the tension and discordance established between how No'u feels labelled when she asserts herself. In this way, the identification of the poem's *you* is seen as having an overarching voice, the voice of public comment. *Protesters gathering in the city* might be the headline on the evening news, but Revilla says no. The ability to name is a powerful one, and this voice, this *you*, has named a group of people who are protecting something as 'protestors', implying *they're* the ones doing wrong, instead of protecting the already harmed from further harm, the already violated from complete annihilation. 'Protest music' is a term given to a certain genre of song. 'Protective poetry' is perhaps the genre of this poem, and the music is heard in the tension Revilla amplifies, addressing a voice that's silenced her.

No'u Revilla is an 'Ōiwi (Hawaiian) poet. As an adult she learnt her own language, a language that had been systematically removed by policies and practices of white Europeans and Americans. The presence of Christian missionaries in Hawai'i has, for the past two centuries, been inextricably linked with the destruction of indigenous ways of life: language, governance, monarchy, self-rule, trade, land and culture. Colonisation often seems like far too easy a word for everything it means. It means war, and in the name of war often blames its victims for their own acts of self-defence.

The religious elements in this poem intrigue me: the smile, for example, is 'shiny as a church'. Revilla honours prayer but doesn't trust everything that calls itself prayer: 'what / kind of prayer could ever be trusted without / evidence of a free tongue?' In a theological critique of this poem, freedom must accompany devotion, and devotion without freedom is an untrustworthy thing because it demands obedience without the possibility of query. The tongue is now the focus, the thing that's used to make the sounds we use to name things. Like some recalcitrant Adam naming things in the Garden of Eden that weren't his to name, this *you* annihilates 'the girl the Native / the water the mountain', justifying such horrors by saying they were 'asking for it'. The choice of strikethrough for these words is, in itself an act of reclamation: where identities are erased, Revilla acknowledges the wound of erasure while also drawing attention to what should never be desecrated: the girl, the Native, the water.

This is a female-voiced resistance to male-dominated white Christianist supremacy. The speaker knows her own powerful protective force: 'Sometimes I dream of / tearing your throat wide open'. But she doesn't. The *you* she speaks to has used violence, and then further justified the violence. The throat-ripping fantasy of Revilla's dream is a certain curiosity about where their words come from. She's keen to know the source of such malicious language. Maybe she's trying to believe that somewhere, deep within a person, there's a place of integrity where truer words can be found. But this voice, in a tone of missionary purity, is not interested in holy things – like land, and people, and place and language – at all. On the contrary, there's only bleeding and the 'wish to desecrate'. No wonder No'u Revilla recalls the tradition of women hiding daggers in their hair; no wonder she praises protection in the face of such aggression.

For months I had been eagerly anticipating the publication of the book *Deaf Republic*, by Ilya Kaminsky. It was released in March 2019, on a day I was flying home from the US to Ireland. I'd not been able to make it to a bookshop before my flight, but the airport bookshop had an impressive selection of poetry. I'd read the book three times before I arrived back in Dublin.

It was Ash Wednesday. I had ashes on my forehead to mark the start of Lent. Flying from Minneapolis to Chicago to Dublin, I wondered how many others would have ashes on their skin – there were hundreds of us.

I always associate this book – a book that pays attention to complicity – with ash on skin, with marks of lamentation made in public.

We Lived Happily during the War

Ilya Kaminsky

And when they bombed other people's houses, we

protested
but not enough, we opposed them but not

enough. I was
in my bed, around my bed America

was falling: invisible house by invisible house by invisible house –

I took a chair outside and watched the sun.

In the sixth month
of a disastrous reign in the house of money

in the street of money in the city of money in the country of money,
our great country of money, we (forgive us)

lived happily during the war.

'We Lived Happily during the War' is the first poem in Ilya Kaminsky's collection *Deaf Republic.* It is a poetry collection, yes, but it's also a story, a drama, a piece of theatre. The opening pages list a cast of characters, as in a play.

Deaf Republic narrates what happens in the fictional city of Vasenka when – at a puppetry show in the town square – soldiers shoot and kill a Deaf boy who had dared to laugh at a public performance of political satire. The community, as a response to this murder, decide not to listen anymore to the soldiers or their authorities; they choose to be a Deaf Republic, coordinating their communication and subterfuge through sign language. Often in literature, deafness is a tired and insulting metaphor, a shorthand for ignorance or stubbornness. Kaminsky is Deaf himself, and in this collection, he uses Deafness as an exploration of resistance.

Vasenka is an everytown. 'We Lived Happily during the War' names America, a place Ilya Kaminsky has lived since his family sought asylum from the Ukranian city of Odessa. In light of the 2022 invasion of Ukraine by Russian forces his words seem particularly pertinent to the ways in which war thrives on the nonchalance of those who have the luxury of not feeling personally implicated. Kaminsky holds residents of any town to scrutiny, implicating readers in the questions of civic life, requiring them to get uncomfortable about their comfort.

in the street of money in the city of money in the country
   of money,
our great country of money

What has money done for this speaker, the poem asks?
It's been a fantasy, a final goal. But it's also been a distrac-
tion: pursuing 'our great country of money' has been a
technique for maintaining apathy in a population, the excuse
they've used for ignoring the war that's been happening all
around them. Meanwhile the spoils of war increase for the
already rich. In the face of this abomination, this poem
laments that nothing more was done: 'we // protested / but
not enough'. Would protest or opposition have changed
anything? That isn't the question this poem asks.

'We Lived Happily During the War' is a devastating poem
about complicity, accompanied by a strange music in the
refrains of *but not enough . . . but not enough* and *my bed
. . . my bed*. The poem is full of tension: will it break apart,
or not? Will there be anyone to sing for the person whose
comfort has now ended? Often, a piece of music will come
to a natural end, where an underlying chord is sounded,
where any listener will sense that the melody has come to
a resolution, a rest. However, in this exquisitely musical
poem, Ilya Kaminsky exposes rather than resolves.

Who is speaking in this short poem? At times it seems
they have a mild voice, almost detached, as seen in the line
'I took a chair outside and watched the sun.' But by the end
of the poem the speaker's '(forgive us)' demands attention.
Why is this voice asking for forgiveness? From whom? Do
they deserve it? I think the speaker is seeking forgiveness

from those who are gone. Underneath the musical register of this speaker is a cruel irony: they are begging forgiveness from the dead, the very people they did not do enough to help while they were alive.

There is a powerful politics of Disability in this collection. In English, phrases like 'I was blind to that' or 'it fell on deaf ears' are problematic but also commonplace. Years ago, when I worked for the Irish Wheelchair Association, I had a boss, Maureen McGovern, a Disabled woman herself and a Disability rights worker. In my first week, she said to me 'Never use my impairment as a metaphor for your ignorance.' She changed my use of language; she helped me think about saying what I meant to say, making me reject flimsy turns of phrase that fall apart once examined. The speaking voice in Ilya Kaminsky's poem can see, hear and move, yet still has chosen ignorance, stubbornness, and moral turpitude; their lack of impairment is no indication of a lack of cowardice.

Many people will be familiar with Martin Niemöller's words:

First they came for the Communists
And I did not speak out
Because I was not a Communist

Then they came for the Socialists
And I did not speak out
Because I was not a Socialist

Then they came for the trade unionists
And I did not speak out
Because I was not a trade unionist

Then they came for the Jews
And I did not speak out
Because I was not a Jew

Then they came for me
And there was no one left
To speak out for me

Martin Niemöller was a Lutheran pastor from Germany, and his words, too, are a reckoning with inaction. Niemöller had initially supported Hitler's rise to power, only later turning against him, ending up in a concentration camp. He was one of the people who was liberated from that camp, and was a public speaker and campaigner for decades afterwards: notably, however, he didn't use his platform to ask for forgiveness, rather to do penance. Ilya Kaminsky highlights that while one person wonders whether they'll survive the day, another is wondering what colour they'll paint the kitchen. In the face of systemic oppression, it's easy for the comfortable to resort to apathy: *what good can I do?* The aim of the poem is not about whether opposition or protest will succeed. Rather, Ilya Kaminsky demonstrates an interest in action: did you protest 'enough'? did you oppose 'enough'?

If a person is a complex being with many stories, then perhaps poetry should be too. There should always be room for more than just one thing to be true in the language of a poem.

Writing the camp
Yousif M. Qasmiyeh

What makes a camp a camp? And what is the beginning of a camp if there is any? And do camps exist in order to die or exist forever?

Baddawi is my home camp, a small camp compared to other Palestinian camps in Lebanon. For many residents, it comprises two subcamps: the lower and the upper camps that converge at the old cemetery. As I was growing up, it was common for children to know their midwife. Ours, perhaps one of only two in the entire camp, was an elderly woman, who died tragically when a wall collapsed on top of her fragile body during a stormy day in the camp. The midwife was the woman who cut our umbilical cords and washed us for the first time. She lived by the main mosque – *Masjid al-Quds* – that overlooked the cemetery. She would always wait by the cemetery to stop those who she delivered on the way to school, to give them a kiss and remind them that she was the one who made them.

The camp is never the same albeit with roughly the same area. New faces, new dialects, narrower alleys, newly constructed and ever-expanding thresholds and doorsteps, intertwined clothing lines and electrical cables, well-shielded balconies, little oxygen and impenetrable silences are all amassed in this space. The shibboleth has never been clearer and more poignant than it is now.

Refugees ask other refugees, who are we to come to you and who are you to come to us? Nobody answers. Palestinians,

Syrians, Iraqis, Kurds share the camp, the same-different camp, the camp of a camp. They have all come to re-originate the beginning with their own hands and feet.

Now, in the camp, there are more mosques, more houses of God, while people continue to come and go, like the calls to prayer emanating at slightly varied times from all these mosques, supplementing, interrupting, transmuting, and augmenting the voice and the noise simultaneously.

Baddawi is a camp that lives and dies in our sight. It is destined to remain, not necessarily as itself, so long as time continues to be killed in its corners.

Yousif M. Qasmiyeh is a poet and translator, based now in England, who was born and grew up in the Baddawi refugee camp in northern Lebanon. It's located near the city of Tripoli, and was established in 1955 for Palestinian refugees. The entire camp is one square kilometre, and in the years since its establishment has expanded up, not out. Tens of thousands of people have arrived at this camp from all over that region, most recently from Syria.

'Writing the camp' comes from a book of the same title, published in 2021: a collection exploring questions of family, place, time and home. To read poetry that directly considers the word *camp* is to engage with the word itself. For many, the word – it can be a verb or noun – connotes summer holidays. But that's a modern usage of the word. The Middle English term *kampe* means a battlefield. The French word for field is *champ.* So *camp* means different things, depending on where you're from: a field to stay a night; a field to fight in.

Here, Qasmiyeh uses the word *camp* – in various configurations – eighteen times. He's chewing the word, trying to make its borders and its strangeness digestible. The borders of this prose poem are fixed: six blocks of writing arranged on the page, all justified down the left and the right like 1km^2 arrangements of language. 'Writing the camp' also means shaping it: the page of this poem is tight with ink, leaving only a little space; the form mimics boundaries.

The word *liminality* comes from *liminis*, a word originally referring to the doorstep or threshold you step over when moving from one room to another; or when standing, perhaps, in the space between two rooms: half in, half out. The concrete nature of the term grounds the concept of liminality in a much more interesting way than its contemporary abstract uses would imply. Qasmiyeh is an explorer of liminality. The Baddawi camp is in Lebanon, but also not. He's written elsewhere about how people speak of going *through* Lebanon to reach the camp, not *to* Lebanon. Baddawi is suspended: half there, half not. Even within the camp, there's a delineation: 'For many residents, it /comprises two subcamps: the lower and the upper camps / that converge at the old cemetery.' Two halves of survival separated by a place to remember the dead. Cemeteries are places to honour those who are no longer present; in a cemetery, we might practice memory – we remember loss too.

Having described the internal informal border that divides the Baddawi camp, the speaker shares the fact that 'As I was growing up, it / was common for children to know their midwife.' The midwife, too, is an attendant of thresholds, the entry point to life and breath, albeit in a temporary camp that's almost seventy years old. How do you measure time in a refugee camp? By how long it's been established? By how long you've been away from the place that you call home? And yet another set of thresholds exist in this place that the speaker calls home:

Refugees ask other refugees, who are we to come to you and who are you to come to us? Nobody answers. Palestinians, Syrians, Iraqis, Kurds share the camp, the same-different camp, the camp of a camp. They have all come to re-originate the beginning with their own hands and feet.

Dialects and languages and multiple belongings all gather, bordering on each other.

The call to prayer begins 'at slightly varied times' in the same small space, home to many populations 'supplementing, interrupting, transmuting, and / augmenting the voice and the noise simultaneously.' In the one camp, different things are happening for different groups whose experience of time is not the same. In Yousif M. Qasmiyeh's hands, poetry itself is an act of resistance: against war, yes, but also against the tendency towards minimalisation. Perhaps that's a reason why the prose poem – poetry that straddles the gap between two literary forms – is such a wise choice for this piece.

There's no idealism in this description of the Baddawi camp: the midwife kisses the children she helped birth as they go to school, then dies tragically under a collapsing wall. The poem tells many stories in one, exploring the philosophical roots of language and place, policies and personhood.

'Writing the camp' ends with a warning, that the camp is destined to remain 'so long as time / continues to be killed in its corners.' Can you kill time? The idea of killing time is often spoken of in terms of leisure, but here, Qasmiyeh speaks about suspended time, and makes that feel like a slow torture, a death. Packing unresolved questions of place and citizenship into temporary camps that turn out to be permanent is, perhaps, a version of killing time. Certainly it's a way that some can forget what's happening: to people, in a place, in their daily experience. The images of internal thresholds inside the camp shift to the threshold between the poem and the reader: how will the reader respond?

Between the ages of ten and twelve, I was learning political poems off by heart, in Irish and English; they were on the school curriculum. They were short, they employed metaphor, mythology, lament, and – fabulously, for a child – some were about ghosts. Thanks to that educational system, it never occurred to me that poetry couldn't address the life of politics; it never occurred to me that the dead had nothing to say about the living; it never occurred to me that poetry couldn't be a call to live differently.

Battlegrounds

Xochitl-Julisa Bermejo

Gettysburg National Military Park

Motorcycles and white tour vans speed
between behemoth granite shafts, shove
my body by their force, leave me roadside
and wandering fields. Little is funny
when you're Chicana and walking
a Civil War site not meant for walking.
Regardless, I ask park rangers and guides
for stories on Mexican soldiers,

receive shrugs. No evidence in statues
or statistics. In the cemetery, not one
Spanish name. I'm alone in the wine shop.
It's the same in the post office, the market,
the antique shop with KKK books on display.
In the peach orchard, I prepare a séance,
sit cross-legged in grass, and hold
a smoky quartz to the setting sun.

I invite the unseen to speak. So many dead,
it's said Confederates were left to rot.
In war, not all bodies are returned home
nor graves marked. I Google 'Mexicans
in the Civil War' and uncover layers
to the Treaty of Guadalupe Hidalgo
and Cinco de Mayo. This is how I meet
ancestors for the first time, heroes

this country decorates in clownish sombreros
and fake mustaches, dishonors for fighting
European empire on shared American land
Power & Money dictate can't be shared.
Years before this, carrying water gallons
up an Arizona mountain ridge to replenish
supplies in a pass known as 'Dead Man's',
I wrote messages on bottles to the living,

scanned Sonoran canyons for the lost,
and knew too many would not be found.
A black Sharpie Virgen drawn on hot plastic
became a prayer: may the next officer halt
before cracking her face beneath his boot,
spilling life on to dirt. No, nothing's funny
when you're brown in a country you're taught
isn't yours, your dead don't count.

For years I've signed up to poetry newsletters, one of which is the Poem-A-Day from the Academy of American Poets website, poets.org. I love this newsletter because it introduces me to new work, often read aloud by the poet, and also provides a short explanatory paragraph – written by that poet – about the themes or writing circumstances of the poem. This poem came in that email a few years ago.

Xochitl-Julisa Bermejo was resident at the Gettysburg National Military Park as the 'Poet in the Park' during the autumn of 2017. In 'Battlegrounds', a poem of five stanzas, the overlap between place and history is explored and exposed: a civil war site, a shop selling KKK literature, an orchard, and an Arizona mountain. All of these are battlegrounds, for the living and for the names of the dead. Time is multi-faceted here: smartphones and tour vans mix with battlegrounds and antique shops. Treaties are alive, yet not everybody knows about them: the Treaty of Guadalupe Hidalgo is the treaty of 1848 (formally called the Treaty of Peace, Friendship, Limits, and Settlement, between the United States of America and the Mexican Republic); and Cinco de Mayo, May 5, marks the victory of Mexican armies over the French in 1862. Alongside these associations of location and history, Bermejo invokes such a pairing herself: inviting the voices of the past into the present through a séance, sitting 'cross-legged in grass, [holding] / a smoky quartz to the setting sun.'

The séance stands in sharp contrast to the antique shop: the shop keeps doorways to the past ajar by profiting from mementoes of oppression; whereas the poet, through a séance, opens a different door – with ritual, using her body, using a mineral from the earth. Combining light, air and space in an orchard she invites 'the unseen to speak.' It's an act against erasure, this ritual, given that there's 'No evidence in statues / or statistics. In the cemetery, not one / Spanish name. I'm alone . . .' The capacity of a community to tell the truth about their past is a test for how the future will be enacted. The poem's speaker isn't interested in 'clownish sombreros / and fake mustaches'. She's interested in what details reveal, and what ritual can too. There's a careful blending of symbol and pragmatism: séances and iconography are combined with Google and water bottles to preserve life.

In a short note she wrote about this poem for the poets.org daily email, Xochitl-Julisa Bermejo said that this poem believes another way of living is possible. I was fascinated by this comment – at first glance it's a heavy poem, a poem about war, the confederacy and the KKK; a poem where Mexican soldiers are unnamed, where people might die of thirst while crossing a border. What in all of this points to a different future? Reading it multiple times, I began to realise that Xochitl-Julisa Bermejo believes that a telling of the past can be a moral call towards enacting a different present and future. Instead of versions of the violent past being sold in shops, she raises names in séances and also – in another time and place – extends the possibility of survival by linking old with new, prayer with water, helping the living live a little longer when death threatens.

That 'setting sun' offers hope too: the future is about to happen somewhere else, and it's a future Bermejo feels like she has a part in. The speaker in the poem is interested in those who will cross Arizona mountain ranges in pursuit of safety, and provides for them – leaving bottles of water sketched with a sign of hope: a Virgen (meaning Virgin in Spanish), an image of culture, prayer, desperation and consolation.

A therapist friend of mine summarised Freud's theory of the 'repetition compulsion' by saying 'what cannot be remembered will be repeated'. There are things to be remembered – in ritual, in story, in commemoration, in art – that can help us be present to the present. 'Battlegrounds' asks: how will you find a way to be a bridge between the past and the present? By glorifying atrocity? Or by searching for stories of the forgotten and making sure that today's forgotten might have the capacity to continue living and to remember themselves? It's a challenge for every museum, every history class, every curriculum. It's a challenge to politicians in how they speak about the past, and it's a question for every person with responsibility in their community: the past is still living, let the living live into the future.

One of the things I love – but also fear – about poetry is that it asks you to name deep truths. It asks you to lament, to remove shallow comforts in order to let the truth of what you wish to say be said. When I write poems, I feel like they ask me questions, and there's no room for deceit – of myself or others.

[Whereas my eyes land on the shoreline]
Layli Long Soldier

WHEREAS my eyes land on the shoreline of, 'the arrival of Europeans in
North America opened a new chapter in the history of Native Peoples.'
Because in others, I hate the act

of laughing when hurt injured or in cases of danger. That bitter hiding.
My daughter picks up new habits from friends. She'd been running,
tripped, slid on knees and palms onto asphalt.

They carried her into the kitchen, s*he just fell, she's bleeding!* Deep red
streams down her arms and legs, trails on white tile. I looked at her face.
A smile

quivered her. A laugh, a nervous. Doing as her friends do, she braved new
behavior, feigned a grin – I couldn't name it but I could spot it. *Stop, my
girl. If you're hurting, cry.*

Like that. She let it out, a flood from living room to bathroom. Then a
soft water pour I washed carefully light touch clean cotton to bandage.
I faced her I reminded,

In our home in our family we are ourselves, real feelings. Be true.
Yet I'm serious when I say I laugh reading the phrase, 'opened a new
chapter.' I can't help my body.

I shake. The realization that it took this phrase to show. My daughter's
quiver isn't new – but a deep practice very old she's watching me;

So often, the arts can be seen as peripheral to the 'real stuff' of political life. '[Whereas my eyes land on the shoreline]' demonstrates the longstanding tradition of political poetry. Layli Long Soldier engages with official governmental documentation, exploring the depths of yearning that define the human condition, but are often denied in political language. In a powerful demonstration of irony, she shows what public language can do, by highlighting how poor public language often is.

Layli Long Soldier's extraordinary book *WHEREAS* is a response to an apology given by Barack Obama in 2009 while he was the US President. The full title of this official apology is over thirty words long: 'Joint resolution to acknowledge a long history of official depredations and ill-conceived policies by the federal government regarding Indian tribes, and offer an apology to all Native peoples on behalf of the United States'. The statement failed on many levels: it was not read out in public by the President; it involved no consultation with Native peoples; there was no opportunity for official response from any representative of the over 560 Indigenous Nations federally recognised by the United States government. The official document – all available online – is structured formally:

Title
Twenty-one statements each beginning with 'Whereas';

each purporting to make a statement of fact
Section 1: Acknowledgement and apology (seven sentences)
Section 2: Disclaimers

Layli Long Soldier's *WHEREAS* includes twenty-one poems – one for each Whereas statement of the document. She responds to the seven sentences of 'acknowledgement and apology' with seven further poems. Finally, the legal disclaimer receives its rejoinder in a poetic one. It is an electrifying study of how to take official documentation and explore its biases, premises and limitations. Exposing the inadequacies of the formal document, Long Soldier asserts dignity where dignity had been denied – yet again – by poorly considered, rushed documentation.

The structure of '[Whereas my eyes land on the shoreline]' is fascinating. The poet's eyes land on the 'shoreline' of the fourth 'whereas' statement of the official document: 'Whereas the arrival of Europeans in North America opened a new chapter in the histories of the Native Peoples'. What follows is a story of a daughter being carried into the kitchen after falling; she's bleeding and is trying to be brave, but the speaker of the poem assures the girl her tears are fine, she can – and should – cry.

Of the many objectionable things in the government's apology is the term 'A new chapter'. That's what a person might say if they get married or move house. Something lovely, or sad, or unexpected: these are new chapters in a life. Genocide, annihilation of language, and degradation of culture and way of life, does not mark the beginning of a chapter. They are acts of war, they are acts of immolation. '[Whereas . . .]' is a withering critique of this misleading government statement, a statement that includes the word *history.* A more correct employment of this word would be that the arriving Europeans sought to turn Native Peoples *into* history. In the body of this poem, 'chapter' is only one of the words reframed by Layli Long Soldier. Others include *land, shoreline, injured, danger, hiding, running, bleeding, deep red streams, trails on white tile, quivered, braved, feigned, a flood, faced, reminded, real, true, serious, shake, practice, old, watching.* Whether showing up policies' poor use of language, or raising the lament through her powerful choice of words, Long Soldier confronts the so-called impartial language of official statements with the reality of how partial it is.

In the story of the poem – a story of learning not to show hurt; a story of how devastating it is to see a daughter who has imbibed the lesson of stifling feeling – the real attention is on lament. 'That bitter hiding' she calls it; hiding meaning concealing, but also meaning a form of punishment. When the speaker sees her daughter, cut and bleeding but trying to hold the tears in, she urges her to cry, to let it all out. To detail this simple story as a counterargument to the language of the arrival of Europeans opening up 'a new chapter in the history of Native Peoples' is to say that lament is a worthwhile endeavour, that there is much to lament, a bleeding that has gone on for centuries, and is not finished yet. The policy seems to wish to assert: *Oh, we've turned the page to the healing process*. Layli Long Soldier asserts that *we haven't even done step one*. The poem declares that lament will not have its terms defined by the very people who caused the lamentation.

Time is a character in so many poems, including this one: here, time is the future, looking back through the daughter: 'very old she's watching me', asking for permission to lament, to rage, to tell the truth in mourning. 'She let it out, a flood from living room to bathroom.' This poem protests the act of censoring emotion.

For European-descended people, it can be hard to hear the laments from people whose cultures, languages and populations have been annihilated as a result of European policy, practice and theft. These stories are an invitation into discomfort, into truth. 'I faced her I reminded, / *In our home in our family we are ourselves, real feelings. Be true.*' What is a lament in poetry? Initially this poem explores the repression of lament: focusing on the story of a girl who needs to cry, who resists crying; of a mother who realises she's resisted crying; of a family line of people who, too, may have resisted crying. Lament speaks through the mother: '*Stop, my girl. If you're hurting, cry.*' Then we see that lament is a revelation of the truth, a refusal to hide, or to act according to other people's imagination of time.

I've spent a lot of my life thinking about the word *belief*. Often, that's been in the context of religion and theology. However, these days I've become more interested in other echoes of this word. So, when working with groups, I've begun giving the prompt: *Tell a very short story about a time when you were believed*. If it's a group that's got enough time and safety, I'll ask the other question underneath that question: *Tell a very short story about a time when you weren't*. I believe in being believed. The opposite of it is a horror.

Miami Airport

Raymond Antrobus

        why didn't you answer me back there?

you know how loud these things are on my waist?

you don't look deaf?

        can you prove it?

                do you know sign language?

ID?

        why didn't I see anyone that looked like you

           when I was in England?

why were you in Africa?

        why don't you look like a teacher?

        who are these photos of?

        is this your girlfriend?

why doesn't she look English?

        what was the address you stayed at?

        what is the colour

           of the bag you checked in?

what was your address again?

        is that where we're going to find dope?

        why are you checking your phone?

can I take your fingerprints?

why are your palms sweating?

you always look this lost?

why did you tell me your bag was red?

how did it change colour?

what colour are your eyes?

how much dope will I find in your bag?

why isn't there dope in your bag?

why did you confuse me?

why did you act strange when there was nothing on you?

would you believe
what I've seen in the bags of people like you?

you think you're going
to go free?

what did you not hear?

This poem is a list of thirty questions; all of them questions asked of Raymond Antrobus by a guard at an airport. Apart from the title – 'Miami Airport' – there is no context given to the questions, so readers are left to fill in the blanks. In that way, the blank space of the poem offers space for the reader's projections. I experience a sense of suffocation, panic and anger, when I read this poem, even though Raymond Antrobus doesn't tell me to feel such things. In fact, at no point do we hear his own voice. Brilliantly, he's written a poem that leaves no space for him, even though there's space everywhere in this poem.

I'm impressed by how this poem is arranged on the page, the way those questions start in strange places on the line. The more I look at the poem, the more I feel that the way Raymond has randomly placed the poem's lines is an attempt to visually represent the chaos of the experience: the guard feels in total control, whereas the person being asked these questions is left bewildered, wondering where the next question is going to come from, whether every question is the final one, how much longer this will go on for.

The poem opens with 'why didn't you answer me back there?', so the poem's begun before it's even begun. Raymond Antrobus is Deaf, and if you read his book, you know this, but the guard doesn't. There's a possibility this poem might have taken a different direction, with the speaker answering that he's Deaf, and then a conversation ensuing that wasn't a barrage of questions. However, that doesn't happen. He's told he doesn't look deaf; asked whether he can prove it; asked if he knows Sign; asked for ID; asked to explain why he doesn't look like the English people the guard chose to notice when on a trip to England.

By question eight, the guard is looking through the speaker's passport – or phone – and asking him about the places he's been. 'Africa'. No passport has a stamp saying *Africa*, a continent of 1.3 billion people and fifty-four independent countries. Still, the question is why he's been to this continent, and 'Africa' is voiced as an accusation. In a reply we can't hear, we assume the answer is that he was teaching there, because the next question is why he doesn't look like a teacher. The guard's questions imply 'I know what English people, Deaf people and teachers look like, and you don't look like any of them them. Why?' The speaker is asked to explain what he's not, why he hasn't done what the guard thinks he's done, why he doesn't fit into the stereotype he's accused of being.

The guard moves onto photographs: who is in them? A girlfriend doesn't look like what the guard thinks English girlfriends should look like. More questions: addresses where he stayed; the colour of his bag; his address again; then a question about dope; then a question about why he's checking his phone; then fingerprints; then he's asked why he's sweating.

'Miami Airport' does not give details about the age, appearance, race or sex of this guard, even though we might hazard guesses. In this way, the guard's identity can be seen to be irrelevant, even whilst the other person's identity is being criminalised. The guard can act with the guarantee of both power and impunity. What is the guard guarding, here? They are the arbiter as to whether someone is Deaf, is British, is telling the truth about their life. This is achieved in a list of thirty unanswered questions. The poem confidently embodies that famous writerly adage of 'Show, don't tell'.

The poem continues: the bag wasn't the colour he had said it was, so the guard asks him why he said it was a different colour. While the poem displays so much of the imagination of the guard, I find myself imagining how difficult it must be to answer plainly, to be accurate, to maintain whatever composure possible, all the while wondering how long this is going to go on for, and what other demonstration of power is going to be wielded.

Towards the end of the poem, the guard seems annoyed that the traveller doesn't fulfil any expectations: they have failed to have dope in their bag, in having an agenda for misremembering the colour of the bag; have failed in being malicious, or having a duplicitous reason for appearing nervous. He is guilty of acting 'strange when there was nothing on [him]', guilty of not having the things in his bag that the guard expects him to have.

Was the guard shouting, or acting nonchalantly? Was the guard bored, or hoping to be noticed by a colleague or supervisor? Was there some kind of audience for this performance? My guess is that the guard, if asked about their behaviour, would say they weren't discriminatory against Deaf British Jamaicans who have visited Africa, but rather 'was doing my job'. This begs the question: what job?

As a white Irishman who travels frequently but is rarely stopped at airports, I recognise the convenience of my own critical response to the guard. My response to this poem has to go deeper than outrage. I wonder when I'm like the guard, where I, too, force my imagination of people onto people; where I look for evidence of the things I've already pre-decided; where I am surprised when people don't fit into my stereotype of them; where I judge my version of my intentions while ignoring the impact of my behaviour; where I use power in the way this guard uses power.

In two final questions the poem's manipulative voice spills beyond the page. The speaker leaves the interrogation, but the penultimate question – 'you think you're going / to go free?' – sounds like a guarantee that all of this will happen again. There's a malice to the final question: 'what did you not hear?'. Deafness is mocked and queried, and a traveller is promised that this treatment will reoccur somewhere else, at someone else's bidding. *Hear that*, the voice of power seems to be saying, and *See you again.*

'Miami Airport' has haphazardly arranged lines, no rhyme, no apparent form, and great vast spaces between its thirty questions. If it were to be arranged in justified lines, it might resemble a questionnaire. But the poem resists that, because the experience was not like something tedious but limited. The usage of such random form is itself a display of power. Sometimes blank space in a poem functions as a way to map what isn't being said; but here, in 'Miami Airport' the poem's blank space functions as a map for what won't be believed.

Growing up, myself and my siblings were often taken on hill walks with my father and his friends. There's an old tradition in Ireland – perhaps elsewhere too – of bringing a flat stone in your pocket as you climb a hill. Along the way are mounds of these stones, little cairns. People bring rocks for all kinds of reasons: as a token of thanksgiving, or to represent a burden, or to embody the weight that grief brings. These piles made from these flat stones commemorate survival, lament and gratitude. They hallow the hillside.

Kulila
Ali Cobby Eckermann

sit down sorry camp
might be one week might
be long long time

tell every little story
when the people was alive
tell every little story more

don't forget 'em story
night time tell 'em to the kids
keep every story live

don't change 'em story
tell 'em straight out story
only one way story

all around 'em story
every place we been
every place killing place

sit down here real quiet way
you can hear 'em crying
all them massacre mobs

sit down here real quiet
you can feel 'em dying
all them massacre mobs

hearts can't make it up
when you feel the story
you know it's true

tell every little story
when the people was alive
tell every little story more

might be one week now
might be long long time
sit down sorry camp

I lived in Australia for four years in my twenties, and have visited many times since. Once, having spoken at a church, a Wurundjeri man – on whose homeland the city of Melbourne stands – asked if I'd ever been Welcomed to Country. In many meetings across Australia there's an *acknowledgement* of country, where an individual of any heritage starts a meeting by acknowledging the traditional custodians of the land and their descendants past and present, acknowledging that the land was never ceded, and thus is in need of a treaty. The word *welcome* is never part of this; only a person who is Indigenous to an area can offer a Welcome to Country. So when the man in the church asked me if I'd been welcomed, I knew what he was telling me, and asking me. I hadn't. I come from a place where land and language have suffered under the weight of colonialism. But now I was in Australia, where Irish people – who had suffered terribly as a result of land-grabbing – were entirely complicit in racism towards Indigenous people. I didn't deserve a Welcome. I said that to my friend. 'Sit down son,' he said. 'Deserving has nothing to do with it.' We sat in a corner of the church. People were milling about, drinking coffee, catching up while the man performed a ritual of Welcome for me. After he'd finished, we spoke for a long time.

Ali Cobby Eckermann is a Yankunytjatjara woman born in Kaurna land in South Australia. She's a renowned poet in her own country, and abroad too. Her poetry often concerns itself with how adoption functioned as part of the eugenicist policies of white Australia. Under these policies, Indigenous children were kidnapped from their families and forced into mission schools, orphanages or adoptive families. The public justification for these crimes was always made under the guise of care, health, religion or education; but those justifications were always known to be hollow. It was white-run powers enacting terror on Indigenous families. Cultures were decimated by 'population reduction', families were put through horror – many families never saw each other again – and Christian religion was mandated in place of established custom and ritual. Children were punished if they spoke their own languages. Australia is a continent, so the various Indigenous populations of that enormous land-mass spoke a wide variety of languages – approximately 250 different languages. Only half of these spoken languages remain, and most of those are endangered.

Some European families knew that the Indigenous child in their household had been abducted. Other times the European family believed the child was an orphan. In Ali Cobby Eckermann's family line there are four successive generations affected by state adoption; sometimes these adoptions were forced, other times manipulated. Generations were impoverished by enforced distance from one other, and that impoverishment was used as a further justification for future forced interventions by the courts.

The title 'Kulila' has the resonance of the word 'Listen' – the poem is a call to listen to the sorry story of a place. It's an invitation to a community ritual: to sit and reckon with what happened. Many conflict commemorations imagine that a weekend, a civic event, an unveiled plaque can fulfil the job of remembering. Behind this imagination is shame, guilt, and a limited view of how time works. Eckermann's poem is a critique of such impoverished imaginations of time: 'might be one week might / be long long time', she writes. She highlights that nobody – especially not the ancestors of the colonising powers – can put a chronological time limit on how long the loss of culture, language, sovereignty, safety, customs and governance can be mourned. What's dead is still dead, whether a decade or a century later. So mourning is a way of life, not just something to be done, then buried, forgotten about. The idea that the annihilation of your people's way of life is a grief that can be moved on from is an imagination of the inheritors of the colonies.

'[T]ell 'em straight out story'. Will it cause pain to tell this story to successive generations? Yes. '[N]ight time tell 'em to the kids / keep every story live'. Telling this particular story of this particular past is important – otherwise the killing parties will have won. It is an initiation into the horrors of what Europeans have done to First Nations peoples – not only in Australia but all over the world. Racism and colonialism *are* burdens, but telling children the truth in your own way – with custom and remembrance and connection to ancestors and practices – is a marking of power and custom, and is a tactic for surviving in a world often filled with repression.

'[D]on't change 'em story / tell 'em straight out story / only one way story // all around 'em story', Eckermann says. There are burdens to be carried, she's saying – let us not be afraid to carry them. Children can cope with stories of the past. It's the deniers who can't. Her poem is an act of narrative resistance.

Years ago, I heard Krista Tippett interview Mercedes Doretti – a forensic anthropologist who works with the remains of Disappeared people in order to tell their story to their surviving family members – who shared that the UN classifies Disappearance as a form of torture. To not know the whereabouts of a family member – whether they're alive or dead, whether they're adopted or buried – is to be a victim of the crime. This is true for people in any country where individuals have been Disappeared in the name of a conflict, or rule, or war. To not know, to have storylines annihilated, to have the possibility of finding truth removed by that truth being denied – this is a torture. Ali Cobby Eckermann proposes that telling the truth is a way to honour the past, to embody what's been removed.

'[E]very place killing place', she writes, then: 'all them massacre mobs'. Modifying 'you can hear 'em crying' to 'you can feel 'em dying', she repeats 'all them massacre mobs'. The lines are short, using a vernacular English rather than the English that was an enforcing tool of oppressive power. In this way Ali has created a poem with a particular music and its own coded language, one that is recognised by those for whom it is an invitation to participation; one that is recognised by those for whom it is an invitation to reparation. There's a brutal music in how these stanzas echo each other – powerful in its capacity to honour the past with ritual; to use ritual as a form of truth-telling.

'[H]earts can't make it up', Eckermann writes. You couldn't make up this kind of massacre. You can't make up for this kind of massacre with the heart. You couldn't invent the need for this kind of remembrance. You can't replace it, either.

I've thought about the word 'reconciliation' for most of my life. It's been part of the political and religious landscapes that have formed me – sometimes because I've seen people practise it; other times because I've been resistant to it.

It's a strange word, reconciliation. What is it? A place? An experience? Something permanent? Something you sense, from time to time, before getting on with the dishes? These days, I tend to think of reconciliation as finding a way to live creatively with tensions that threaten to undo me. For me, poetry has been necessary in finding this creative tension.

reconciliation

Jónína Kirton

how will I reconcile myself?
the Icelander and the Métis
the settler and the Indigenous
an ally to myself
since birth flung across a chasm
I often wonder am I to forever be
the way across
weak anchors at each end
my spine a flexible deck
load-bearing
and within my cables too much tension
as some try to cross
we all swing wildly
in each other's steps
without safety nets
the waves of emotion
threaten us all
and then there are times
that both sides seek to disown
to cut my cords
let me fall to the rushing
waters below
maybe one day I will just float away
see where the water takes me
but not today
today I will rebuild
this time no quick fixes   no steel cables
                or wooden planks
no rust   no rot

no nails necessary
but rather the slow growth of twisted roots
from ancient trees
the way across a path
made of grandfather
grandmother stones
I will become a self-sustaining structure
gain strength over time
a living root bridge that lasts five hundred years

'reconciliation' begins with a question: 'how will I reconcile myself?' This is not reconciliation to another person – 'how can I be reconciled *to them*? – but about the speaker's relationship to herself. Many poems centre on the question of 'Who am I?' but here we have a slant to that query. Who can I be? this poem asks, and because of a split self, the speaker of the poem searches for an image of a bridge that will support her need to reconcile her mixed heritages.

Jónína Kirton is a Canadian poet of Métis and Icelandic heritage. Métis are a distinct Indigenous group who have both Indigenous and European ancestry – 'métis' is the French word for 'mixed'. In Canada there are particular areas, slightly north of Manitoba, especially, that have a long and distinct connection with Icelanders.

A bridge is a feat of engineering. How much of a load can it bear? How deep does it need to be anchored on each side? What modifications to the land on either side of a bridge are necessary? As Jónína Kirton imagines a bridge between Métis and Icelander culture she recognises the danger of using a typical bridge as a metaphor. Anchors weaken the earth, and the bridge might 'swing wildly'. Were she to build a bridge between Iceland and Canada, what safety nets would such a feat of engineering demand, she wonders? Then there's those waves, those 'rushing / waters below'. Such a bridge fails even the imagination: open to structural failures and also attacks:

enemies who'd cut supportive cables. Threats above and below; threats from structures, threats from others. There's a sense of crisis in the poem. It's clever to use this metaphor – a stretched and perhaps flimsy bridge – in order to speak about feeling personally stretched, at risk of collapse, or attack.

The crisis culminates at the end of the first section: 'maybe one day I will just float away / see where the water takes me'. Is this abandonment? Or giving up, or ending? The tensions Jónína holds are tensions that go to the very fibre of existence.

A linebreak, between two *today*s, begins to address the crisis. In a poem about unbridgeable places a break is used in order to move the poem towards strength. The poetic form itself implies that not everything that's separated needs to be split. A new way of holding split selves together is considered: 'today // today I will rebuild'.

In the second section, rather than abandon the idea of a bridge, Kirton abandons the idea of *building*, imagining instead a bridge that grows. Once, in a public reading I found online, she shared how she researched bridges from around the world, then landed on living root bridges found in India; bridges made not of steel, but of the roots of trees stretched across chasms. The oldest of these bridges is thought to be five hundred years old. Something living – a tree – can be held in the earth in a way that allows the earth and the plant to be mutually sustaining. A living root bridge is part of the earth, spans the chasms of the earth, and *lives*; it is not just a means to an end, rather it's a breathing thing itself. Where does one tree end and another begin? The answer is that something new is created in the in-between. In the zero-sum game of having to cut off one of her identities, Kirton rejects the binary choice, instead seeing her body as a type of living bridge, nurtured by the earth of two places, sustained by both, alive across its entire span.

Many of Jónína's poems are a search for self, or even a reclamation of a self. She published her first poetry collection at the age of sixty. Against a backdrop of ageism, misogyny and identity erasure, her poetry argues for, asserts and creates self-narration.

Many people might remember learning about metaphor in poetry classes at school. Kirton says that her experience is of *being* a bridge; not being *like* a bridge. She's using the concrete image of a bridge and creating a direct poetic line between those structures and the circumstances of her life and identities. She searches for the right kind of bridge to use – in this way, she's feeling for the right metaphor. Bridges are walked on, put under stress, stretched. Supported yes, but under strain. Kirton is in need – physically, as well as emotionally and culturally – of a new way to describe her multiple-cultured life. The poem models a creative way of self-support: in a time of difficulty, pay attention to the images that come to mind; study them, research them – it might be that your intuition's landing on something more supportive than you think.

'reconciliation' responds to a binary choice – *choose one identity, reject the other* – and replaces singularity with multiplicity. Jónína Kirton's poem is an act of defiance, imagination, research and hospitality. It is an act of reconciliation.

I used to think that poetry – and religion, too – was about describing the transcendent; the things you couldn't put your hands on. But these days, I find myself more and more interested in language that pays attention to tangible things. Poems that try to be about everything often end up being about nothing, but poems that pay attention to one thing can have much more to say.

All Bread

Margaret Atwood

All bread is made of wood,
cow dung, packed brown moss,
the bodies of dead animals, the teeth
and backbones, what is left
after the ravens. This dirt
flows through the stems into the grain,
into the arm, nine strokes
of the axe, skin from a tree,
good water which is the first
gift, four hours.

Live burial under a moist cloth,
a silver dish, the row
of white famine bellies
swollen and taut in the oven,
lungfuls of warm breath stopped
in the heat from an old sun.

Good bread has the salt taste
of your hands after nine
strokes of the axe, the salt
taste of your mouth, it smells
of its own small death, of the deaths
before and after.

Lift these ashes
into your mouth, your blood;
to know what you devour
is to consecrate it,
almost. All bread must be broken
so it can be shared. Together
we eat this earth.

Margaret Atwood's poem 'All Bread' is a work of four stanzas. The first is located in the primordial field, with crops growing up amidst soil, cow shit and the corpses of dead animals. The second stanza is set in a kitchen somewhere, bread rising in the heat of an oven. The third stanza is located in a mouth. Whose mouth? Somebody's; everybody's, perhaps. This bread tastes of salt and heat as well as the earth in which the wheat was grown. The final stanza functions almost like a summons, like an agnostic call to a material sacrament: 'to know what you devour / is to consecrate it, / almost.' Bread, here, is an offering to the world. For consumption.

'All Bread' resists the idea of bread as a transcendent image; it's only 'almost' consecrated by being lifted to the mouth. It's a poem of phenomenal materiality: dark earth, dung, moss, corpses and the bits of corpses left behind after the ravens are done with them. Even in an age of hyper-hygiene, Margaret Atwood lets us know that the salt from the hands of the eater – and perhaps the kneader, or anyone else who has touched the bread – is making its way into their mouth and body. It's got death in it, this bread, as well as life.

By paying such attention to the material, edible thing, Margaret Atwood asserts that the tangible and surface are neither flimsy nor shallow, in life or in poetry. The here-and-now is full enough of life and death to be sufficient as a symbol for meaning.

In Richard Holloway's book *Stories We Tell Ourselves*, he quotes a scientist who, when asked how to make bread from scratch, said: 'Well, first you have to invent the universe.' I loved that line, and thought how prescient it was in an age where authentic handcrafted anything is being sold as if it were created *ex nihilo* by an individual. There's a harsh reminder in 'All Bread' of life and death (our own, and other people's): even fertile places like soil are only fertile because of dead things decomposing, releasing everything that kept them alive in order to keep the cycle going. The poem doesn't shrink from death, and nor does it shrink from hunger: 'the row / of white famine bellies / swollen and taut' is a gruesome depiction of preventable starvation; and the words 'in the oven' also call attention to human atrocity.

The 'All' of the title and first word, together with 'Live burial', 'before and after' and 'Lift' all strike me as liturgical language. But for every time the poem sounds like a secular eucharistic feast, it also has echoes of a recipe, that timeless thing where someone asks, 'How do you make this?' Words like 'packed' and 'nine strikes' and 'good water' and 'four hours' could be lifted from the pages of any recipe book. 'Salt' later on, too, and that 'moist cloth'. The poem is a recipe, but also a kind of creed.

I'm getting more agnostic with years, and so the interview between Margaret Atwood and Bill Moyers in which she describes herself as a 'strict agnostic' has been a source of great intellectual and personal comfort for me. In a thought experiment, Moyers asks her if she'd do away with the hunger for God if she could (what an odd question). Her answer is that no, she wouldn't, because to do so would also be to eliminate language. Language is a form of longing, I hear then, and so is prayer; whether fixed to a traditional theology or not. All human cultures have demonstrated the desire for some transcendence: rejection of a religious doctrine does not undo the yearnings of the heart for meaning. 'Lift these ashes / into your mouth, your blood', the speaker of the poem urges, turning from transcendence to embodiment.

Fifteen years ago, I went with two friends to a house by a beach for a short holiday. The two friends were Catholic priests. Every day we sat around the kitchen table, and they took it in turns to say Mass. There was neither flourish nor funkiness about those liturgies – the words were said according to the book – and the memories of those celebrations of the sacrament are more intimate to me than anything I've attended in a cathedral or monastery. At that stage of my life I was desperate to become a priest, but Pope Benedict had just issued an edict that what he called 'men with homosexual tendencies' wouldn't be allowed. I felt like I'd been dumped by God. But here I was, around a small table with two friends, both of them inside the house I so desperately wanted to be admitted to.

I realised, eventually, that I needed to reexamine what I understood the word *priest* to mean, not only as a noun, but as a verb. There is a notable absence of a priest function in Margaret Atwood's poem, and I think that's the point. The poem says: here is something that will keep you alive, and it grew in soil that was nurtured by death; here is the necessity of sharing; here's the taste of salt from skin. If, amongst these four stanzas, there's a priest in the poem, it's death, and all the life that's nurtured by it.

'All Bread' does not answer the existential anxieties of the human condition. Is there something more than what we can observe? We don't know, despite our yearnings. But this poem does address the question of whether we can make something more of the here-and-now. 'All bread must be broken / so it can be shared'. This is a doctrine entirely embedded in the body and the body's hungers. There is no sentimentality. There is a community who shares hunger, and who can 'Together / . . . eat this earth.'

I once spoke to a group in London called COJAM: Community of Jews and Muslims. We had a full day together and everybody had brought food to share. At lunch a few of the members arranged the meal. While they were doing that, others moved to a corner of the room next to the windows, faced Mecca and began their prayer. There was the smell of food, and the sound of whispers from the cooks. There was the rustle of fabric against fabric as people embodied their devotion. There was the sound of prayers recited just under the breath.

If I try, I can remember that ten minutes in my body. I return to that memory like a favourite cathedral.

Prayer

Faisal Mohyuddin

you cleanse   the uncovered
regions   of your body
then stand   at the foot
of prayer   mats facing

    the qibla   unfasten
    your cluttered   mind
    from the tangible   hold of secular
    trances   bow down

before   the cascading
glow of God's mercy   submit
to a centripetal   course toward the gates
of a more perfect   emptiness

    here   now
    you can plunge   into the most secluded
    chamber of the soul   commune
    with your share   of the universe's

initial burst of   light eternal light
housed within the lamp   of mystery
waiting   to be
beheld   five times a day

The first thing I notice about 'Prayer' is its form. Ten tiny stanzas arranged in two columns. How could the shape of this poem be described? When I initially read this poem I wondered if I was looking down at prayer mats from a height. Then I found myself wondering about the five pillars of Islam. Then I looked at the space between these elegant verses and thought how only smoke – or incense – could fill the space between them. The shape of this poem is one that invites us to look at the blank space; perhaps that itself is one of the messages of the poem, that prayer is what's found in the in-between.

'Prayer' contains no punctuation: no periods or full stops, no commas, no em dashes, no colons or semi-colons. Reciting these ten stanzas aloud – you read from left to right across the gaps – you're left wondering where to take a breath. Taking this poem into your body you must meet it with the pace of your own breath: a poem about prayer brings you into the economy of prayer.

The poem's first focus is the body: it describes the preparation for prayer in the Islamic tradition, where uncovered parts of the body – the face, the hands, the feet – are washed. The person stands in prayer, facing the qibla, the direction of the Sacred Mosque in Mecca.

Physical preparation invites inner preparation and the form Faisal uses lends itself to spaciousness and a lack of rush: the distance between 'you cleanse' and 'the uncovered' shows how preparation for prayer is itself a prayer. 'unfasten // your cluttered // mind' the poem instructs, invoking multiple meanings of the verb 'unfasten' – make a little space from the busyness of the day, yes, but also, let yourself be un-fast. Slow down.

The speaker of this poem knows how the body is the house of prayer, but also the house of distraction, describing the 'tangible // hold of secular // trances'. The word *trance* comes from the Latin *transire* meaning 'go across'. I find myself thinking of how tiring every day can sometimes be; and how it can be tiring even to think of doing restorative things like prayer. In the place of pursuits, Faisal Mohyuddin's poem suggests a kind of prayer that is at once full of stillness and also full of movement: verbs like 'stand', 'facing', 'submit', 'housed', and 'waiting' make me think of composure; whereas 'cascading', 'plunge', 'commune', 'burst' and 'beheld' suggest movement, or perhaps exchange. The *doing* of this poem, then, brings practice into conversation with stillness; a stillness that contains exchange. Nothing is rushed, but nothing is static, either. What is still and alive all at once? The flame of a candle perhaps, or a lamp, or starlight, or the eyes of someone looking at you as you look at them.

On a flight leaving Ireland once, I noticed that the young man beside me blessed himself – making the sign of the cross on his body by touching his head, his torso, his right then his left shoulder – as the plane took off from Dublin airport. When we landed a few hours later, he and I happened to be chatting and I noticed – as simple as a breath – how he blessed himself again. What was this? A prayer: unforced, unembarrassed, unhurried and unimposing. To a critical eye, his gestures might be meaningless: if the plane was going to crash it would have crashed and his prayer would do nothing to stop that. But to make that critique, I think, is to miss the purpose of prayer, whether that of my neighbour on a plane, or my neighbour in the poem: the point is the practice, the using of the body to turn towards something that sustains the inner life.

Not all prayers name the god they turn towards, and Faisal Mohyuddin's poem is modest about the power of language to describe what is indescribable, only standing at the 'gates'. God's mercy is described as a 'cascading // glow'. If there is poetry in the space between these verses, then there is also poetry in God being named a 'perfect // emptiness'. Prayer comes from the 'most secluded // chamber of the soul' and in that place is a small corner of the universe's original fire. How can a person's silent practice be a container for an echo of the big bang? *Like this*, Faisal seems to say, washing his hands, standing at the foot of a mat, bowing, reciting, recalling, submitting, rejoicing, silencing, *like this*.

A poem of prayer holds contradictions in its language, perhaps what a devotee might call a divine contradiction: a finite body can turn toward infinity; God is emptiness and everything; the eternal light can be housed in a lamp. Two simple domestic words – *house* and *lamp* – appearing as a verb and a noun. Is this poem suggesting that the home of God is in the lamp of the heart? Does this poem imagine that physical gestures can move a person towards that which is untouchable? I think so. This is a poem of devotion, not demand; a poem of care, not coercion. 'Prayer' is not a defence of dogma, rather it is an invitation to explore mystery: the mystery of emptiness and substance; the mystery of light and dark; the mystery of the infinite and the tangible. Faisal Mohyuddin houses prayer in a quietened body turned toward eternity.

I've been to many religious services where the priest recites a poem as part of a liturgy. Many poems have the echoes of prayer, but they resist being summaries of religion. The prayer-poems I love most sidestep creed, using fresh language to explore the strange mysteries of being alive.

from *The Book of Hours*
Rainer Maria Rilke
(Trans. Mark S. Burrows)

I love the dark hours of my being,
for they deepen my senses;
in them as in old letters I find
my daily life already lived
in holy words, so soft and subdued.

From them I've come to know that I have room
for a second life, timeless and wide.

And at times I'm like the tree, ripe and rustling,
standing above the dead boy's grave,
gathering him in its warm roots,
fulfilling the dream he'd lost
in sorrows and songs.

In the woods, on the 22nd of September.

Rilke (1875-1926) is one of those poets whose names I'd heard for so long I'd become intimidated by everything I didn't know about him. I knew he was a central European poet who wrote in a German that could never be adequately translated into English. I'd heard Krista Tippett speak about Rilke regularly on her podcast *On Being*. During a long winter lockdown my friend Pat suggested we meet on Zoom every Sunday to discuss a book. She's been a fan of Mark Burrows' translations of Rilke for years, so she recommended that I purchase a copy. It came with a helpful intro, both about Rilke's work and about the circumstances in which he wrote *The Book of Hours* (*Das Stunden-Buch*). I was hooked.

A book of hours is like a prayer book, something nuns and monks use for their morning, midmorning, noon, afternoon, early evening, evening and night prayers. A book of hours gives a layout for monastic prayers: normally a reflection on a psalm, a reading, a prayer of request, a prayer of confession, a prayer of praise and blessing; an amen. Rilke's *Book of Hours* is an extraordinary echo of that genre of daily prayer book.

Rilke had a lifelong connection with the Russian-born psychoanalyst Lou Andreas-Salomé. They were lovers for a few years, and remained friends until Rilke's death. She brought him to Russia, introducing him to new literatures, and was his intellectual and artistic companion throughout his life. She too had a huge literary output, writing about

God, the erotic, literature and philosophy. From September to October 1899, enthralled by his early Russian trips, Rilke began writing a prayer book in the persona of a Russian monk. This was to become the first part of *The Book of Hours*. The prayers were intimate, urgent, spacious and shocking. They were prayers to God, yes, but in a language that was reciprocal and engaging, where the God's yearning seemed to be as strong as the poet's.

Rilke was a young man while writing these poems, not yet twenty-five. Two more bursts of writing followed in the subsequent years, and what's known now as *The Book of Hours* was published in 1906. The first batch of poems from this collection had marginalia around them, almost like notes in a prayer book, written in the persona of that imagined Russian monk. Often, the notes are about the weather, or the time of day, or what's occupying or delighting the monk's mind. Most of these notes are placed after the poem, sometimes before, sometimes both. They're beautiful and strange. I love Mark Burrows' inclusion of these marginalia.

This poem is the fifth in *The Book of Hours* and opens with one of Rilke's characteristic and extraordinary statements:

I love the dark hours of my being

For Rilke, darkness is a place of enlightenment; storms are too. He is a poet interested in bridging gaps: between darkness and light; between God and humanity; between eros and prayer; between self and others; between now and eternity. These dark hours deepen his senses. Darkness, for Rilke, is holy. It is a place of knowledge, sustenance and containment.

Rilke was writing these early poems in the autumn of 1899. Turns of the century are often imagined as the birth of a new era, an occasion to enter a young century with a fresh sense of imagination and possibility. Rilke's poems mix the ecstatic – 'I have room / for a second life, timeless and wide' – with caution: the upcoming century held as much foreboding for him as it did promise for others.

There are many translations of Rilke into English. Some translations omit this poem, or omit the image of the dead boy's grave. I've always wondered if it's due to the shocking image of a tree growing above a dead boy's grave, holding him, mothering him almost – 'gathering him in its warm roots'. Who speaks about a dead boy like this? What dead boy? How can this be a prayer? To whom? Is God the tree? Who does that make us?

Rilke had been shipped off to military school as a young boy, and the ache for tenderness, even sensuality, is evident in his letters and poems, alongside an unexpected capacity to be brutal about reality. This early experience of absence turned him toward yearning and somehow, in his art, Rilke seems to find the fulfilment of his longing. What matters is that you pray, nothing else, Rilke suggests. Sometimes I've found his point of view intensely comforting; other times I've found it irritating. If this is a prayer, to whom is it addressed? Is God in the darkness of the hours, in the experience of the senses, in the ritual of finding a rhythm to a life, or in the imagination that allows 'room / for a second life, timeless and wide'? Maybe God is the seed that led to the tree, and the self is the thing that finds the second life in the branches reaching to heaven. Maybe God is the embrace of the sad boy in its warm roots, holding together what nobody else could hold together. Maybe the boy is Rilke.

The poem is set in the woods, in late September. Autumntime. Perhaps leaves are beginning to turn, perhaps the air carries the inevitability of change at summer's end. What's clear is that Rilke's persona of the monk is in the woods, seeing trees lifting their branches to the sky, writing poems about dark hours and possibility and the things that lie in our roots. The boy from this poem had a dream, but lost it in sorrows and songs. Maybe Rilke is comforting himself. He's still a young man, in the throes of an intense affair with Lou Andreas-Salomé. Love brings out intimacies in us: old desires, old wounds. Maybe the boy under the tree is the child who was shipped off to military school. Rilke had been raised in grief, too: his older sister died, so when he was born he was in her wake, and his mother dressed him as a girl for a number of years. René was his name before it was changed by his lover to Rainer; René meaning *reborn*. In a certain sense this could be seen as a poem written by a person who knew about the necessary burdens of death and endings, who knew – or hoped – it was possible to mother yourself, who trusted longing as much as fulfilment.

Who *doesn't* have a story about laughing at the wrong time; alone, or next to a friend whose silent laughter was contagious?

I was once in an earnest prayer meeting. The speaker decided to riff on a New Testament text about humanity being 'God's handiwork' but instead of saying we were God's *organism*, they said we were God's *orgasm*. I was nineteen. Even now, I can remember the shudders in my body as I tried to hold my laughter in. I did not succeed.

How Prayer Works
Kaveh Akbar

Tucked away in our tiny bedroom so near each other
the edge of my prayer rug covered the edge of his, my
brother and I prayed. We were 18 and 11 maybe, or 19
and 12. He was back from college where he built his own
computer and girls kissed him on the mouth. I was barely
anything, just wanted to be left alone to read and watch
The Simpsons.

We prayed together as we had done thousands of times,
rushing ablutions over the sink, laying our janamazes out
toward the window facing the elm which one summer
held an actual crow's nest full of baby crows: fuzzy, black-
beaked fruit, they were miracles we did not think to
treasure.

My brother and I hurried through sloppy postures of
praise, quiet as the light pooling around us. The room
was so small the twin bed took up nearly all of it, and
as my brother, tall and endless, moved to kneel, his foot
caught the coiled brass doorstop, which issued forth a
loud *brooong.* The noise crashed around the room like a
long, wet bullet shredding through porcelain.

My brother bit back a smirk and I tried to stifle a snort
but solemnity ignored our pleas – we erupted, laughter
quaking out our faces into our bodies and through the
floor. We were hopeless, laughing at our laughing, our
glee an infinite rope fraying off in every direction.

It's not that we forgot God or the martyrs or the Prophet's holy word – quite the opposite, in fact, we were boys built to love what was in front of our faces: my brother and I on the floor draped across each other, laughing tears into our prayer rugs.

This poem of Kaveh Akbar's comes from a collection titled *Pilgrim Bell*. There are six poems of that name throughout the collection, and many of the poems include the sound of a bell, or something like the sound of one. The book itself is some kind of call to prayer, to attention. These poems have their attention turned towards the call of this bell, and also what it means to be in this world, with all its prejudices, privileges, possibilities, hatreds, wars, and wonders. In 'How Prayer Works', while two brothers are turning towards prayer, they're also turning towards their lives.

There's a gorgeous interplay between distance and nearness in this poem. The brothers – eleven and eighteen we hear, or maybe twelve and nineteen – feel far apart in years. Seven years is a long time when you're in that decade of your life. One was 'barely anything' but the other was 'tall and endless'; one is just waking up to himself, the other has moved away to college and its freedoms, leaving behind an empty bed in a tiny bedroom where the younger brother imagines the older brother's life: computers and kissing. *Back home I share a bedroom with my little brother*, you can imagine the older brother saying – or maybe avoiding saying – to his friends at college. Anyway, he's back now, sharing this small space with his young brother, the future poet. 'How Prayer Works' is a slant way of remembering, drawing the distant past near: at the beginning, these brothers are separated by those seven years; by the end, they're draped across each other in laughter.

The brothers face the window as they pray. Through the window are elm trees, whose branches housed baby birds. Past these trees is Mecca. The brothers' prayer rugs touch, like curtains do when they're pulled together. These are not the prayers of the pious: 'We prayed together as we had done thousands of times, / rushing ablutions over the sink'. Prayer, here, is hurried, but the prayers are still said. In this poem, prayer is the un-ironed sweater you throw on when you're not trying to impress anyone. And in that everyday devotion, that lack of pretence, there's intimacy.

What are you praying *for* when you're praying? You're praying in unity with Muslims in your own time zone, a move of supplication and praise circling around the planet like a slow wave. Kaveh's gorgeous poem portrays prayer as practice rather than plea. This is how the body prays, not just the mind. You – and millions of others – stand; you kneel; you bow; you say the words. This is 'How Prayer Works'.

It was only when I read this poem that I noticed that I, too, have coiled brass doorstops in my house. I stood and thwonged one the other morning. A friend and her four-year-old son were staying with me. 'What does that sound like?' I asked him. 'A fart,' he answered. This noise interrupts the prayers of the brothers. The *brooong* of the coiled brass doorstop has been sounded by the lengthy brother in a tiny room. They try not to laugh, which is of course, the sure way to make laughter happen. Solemnity – a thing of the mind – has been shirked off, and laughter – a thing of the body – has arrived. Why is the sound of that doorstop funny? Who knows. The thing is, it *was* funny, and they laughed, and then laughed at their laughter: their 'glee an infinite rope fraying off in every direction.' A rope to where? To each other perhaps, to their connection, to their bodies, to their youth, to their sibling-hood: continuing and fraying, fraying and continuing.

In 'How Prayer Works' parents are notably absent. Adults are implied – the house; the requirement to say prayers; the purchasing of the curtains, mats and beds – but adults are in the fabric of this poem, rather than the action.

A prose poem plays with the seeming contradiction between prose and poetry. And this, I think, is one of the things that Kaveh Akbar is doing by using this shape for this poem. Perhaps people think laughter and prayer shouldn't mix; or sloppiness and devotion. In form and content this poem disagrees. Words like 'ignored' and 'erupted' and 'hopeless' and 'fraying' and 'tears' occur in the poem, together with words that can express laughter, devotion, brotherhood and happenstance. 'How Prayer Works' is anything but frivolous. It is a joyful response to the serious question of how to hold things together: with practice, with companionship, with repetition, with openness to the world, with spontaneity, laughter and freedom, even in a small room of restriction.

'How Prayer Works' presents as five justified blocks of text. These five stanzas build on the other: the first stanza locates us in the small room, and tells us about the brothers; the second orients us to their prayers, the direction they face and everything they see and do not see; the third stanza speaks about their bodies in prayer and the sound of the *brooong*; the fourth sees them erupting into uncontrollable laughter. Then the final, the fifth: a stanza that moves into theology.

In a poem with this title you might expect some explor-ation about God's action in the world – a defence or critique of intervention. However, the final stanza stays with the boys' laughter, casting aside any imagination that their joy was a distraction from the serious work of prayer: 'quite the opposite, in fact, we were boys built / to love what was in front of our faces'. Here, prayer works by being human, by being embodied, by holding things together, by opening your eyes to the world: baby birds and surprising sounds, unexpected joy, brothers being brothers through their years of change. Maybe somebody prayed that the brothers would get on during this visit. This poem is the answer: here's how prayer works.

Ever since I was a child, I've been fascinated and sometimes frightened by stories of the Bible. It's been the literature of my life. It has been a captor and it's been a spark for my imagination.

Any ancient text can be a terror or a talisman, the key is in how you read it. As I've got older, I've turned more to poets than theologians to help me find inroads into religious literature. The more I think of the Bible as art, rather than obligation, the wilder it's become; the more curious I've felt in the face of strange texts, the more seriously I can take them.

Of Course She Looked Back

Natalie Diaz

You would have, too.
From that distance the shivering city
fit in the palm of her hand
like she owned it.

She could've blown the whole thing –
markets, dance halls, hookah bars –
sent the city and its hundred harems
tumbling across the desert
like a kiss. She had to look back.

When she did she saw
pigeons glinting like debris above
ruined rooftops. Towers swaying.
Women in broken skirts
strewn along burned-out streets
like busted red bells.

The noise was something else –
dogs wept, roosters howled, children
and guitars popped like kernels of corn
feeding the twisting blaze.

She wondered had she unplugged
the coffeepot? The iron?
Was the oven off?
Her husband uttered, *Keep going*.
Whispered, *Stay the course*, or
Baby, forget about it. She couldn't.

Now a bursting garden of fire
the city bloomed to flame after flame
like hot fruit in a persimmon orchard.

Someone thirsty asked for water.
Someone scared asked to pray.
Her daughters or the crooked-legged angel,
maybe. Dark thighs of smoke opened
to the sky. She meant to look
away, but the sting in her eyes,
the taste devouring her tongue,
and the neighbors begging her name.

In 'Of Course She Looked Back' Natalie Diaz revisits the story of the Destruction of the City of Sodom. That story, found in the nineteenth chapter of Genesis, the first book of the Bible, is about messengers, hospitality and violence. Briefly: angels arrive at the city of Sodom and are given hospitality by Lot, a prominent man in that city. These angels – the word angel means *messenger* in many languages – have come with a message for the city: change your ways. Lot is the only one in the city to show them hospitality: the rest of the city rejects them, so much so that the text says that *all the men of the city, from the oldest to the youngest, crowded outside the house of Lot, calling for the messengers to be brought out, so they could be brutalised by all of them.* The angels then set out their plan to destroy the city, telling Lot how to save himself, along with his family. *When you leave the city, don't look back*, they said. Lot's whole household escaped Sodom. But Lot's wife, whose name we don't know, turned back to watch the destruction of her city. For this, she was turned into a pillar of salt.

It's been a story of power and horror for centuries. For a long time – because of the townsmen's threat to rape the angels – the story of Sodom has been told as a story of sex between men. However, the text of the Bible is clear: the sin of Sodom was the sin of inhospitality. Of course the entire male population of the city wasn't gay: the men of Sodom were using a type of violence that has been demonstrated in many different cultures and contexts – rape as a weapon. There's nothing gay about that, but there's plenty male about it. I was terrorised by this story as a teenager; being told that it demonstrated God's eternal stance towards people like me. The story was used as a text of control by those who interpreted it for me, and back then, I didn't know it was possible to explore the story with imagination. Natalie Diaz does, though, and she enters the story through the point of view of Lot's unnamed wife – the woman who fled a burning city but dared to look back.

The title is also the opening line, and, when reading it aloud, you move seamlessly from the title to the body of the poem: 'Of Course She Looked Back // You would have, too.' A story of ethical disobedience is about to unfold. In the skilful art of Natalie Diaz, we are looking back at Sodom through Lot's wife's eyes, and we're given her point of view; we see what a woman sees – a woman whose life has been upturned by the violence of men and angels. We see things in the City of Sodom not deemed important enough for the biblical story. The escapees are far enough away that the city can be covered by the palm of a hand. At this distance, Lot's wife is almost like a god – she could blow the city away, or kiss it. Which will she do? She's no god, but even in this powerlessness, she looks with love. She doesn't cover her view with a palm, or an eyelid, or by a turned back.

The story of Sodom's destruction (alongside its sister city, Gomorrah) is told by the victors: those who left, those who heeded the story of the angels. But the story of victors is often to be doubted. In Natalie Diaz's reframing point of view, we are brought into another way of looking at the story, but also, importantly, another way of looking at any story. This poem is an invitation to consider other destructions –

of cities, of peoples, of languages, of livelihoods – from the point of view of the destroyed. By modernising the story (oh, those coffeepots, and electricals, and ovens) Diaz brings the biblical story into a contemporary telling: this isn't about one story that happened once; this is about something that happens, and has happened, many times.

Natalie Diaz was born and raised in the Fort Mojave Indian village in Needles, California, in what is now called the United States. She is Mojave and an enrolled member of the Gila River Indian Tribe. She's also a linguist and has worked with the last speakers of Mojave, directing a language revitalisation programme. She attends to the edges of destruction. By taking on the voice of Lot's wife, she is honouring the integrity of a woman who turned around to face her city's end, despite being instructed not to do so. In 'Of Course She Turned Back' Lot's wife is praised alongside all the others who disobey orders in order to bear witness to their homeland.

The story of Sodom is a story about how men brutalise others – people of any gender – instead of facing their own hostility. This happens over and over again, in wars as well as in places that say that they're in peace. Because this story has been used as a terrorising tool for LGBTQI+ people, this poem's reclamation of Lot's wife's gaze is a queer corrective to a tool of oppression. By offering tenderness towards this destroyed and despised city, Diaz exposes and undoes old ways of interpreting this story. If you take the idea that God – or God's angels – destroyed the city, then the violence is minimised. Through Lot's wife's eyes, however, we see the hustle and bustle of a recognisable city: markets, halls, bars, harems, birds, towers, women, the fashions of the day, stray dogs, livestock. Everything destroyed, along with 'children / and guitars [who] popped like kernels of corn'. This point of view is not just one of tenderness towards a city, but also one of accusation towards whatever system justifies such horror and violence.

In the story of Sodom, the inhabitants of the city are mostly referred to as 'the men of Sodom'. In Natalie Diaz's poem, however, we hear about 'Women in broken skirts / strewn along burned-out streets / like busted red bells'; we hear children; we hear that this is a place where music was played, where animals lived. Sodom was a place of domesticity: coffee and iron and clothes and cooking; a place of agriculture, where there would've been persimmon orchards; a place where people are – like all people – thirsty and turning to prayer. This poem asserts that women of Sodom were citizens too. Did God ignore their virtue while judging the city by the violence of men? If so, God deserves to be stared down. Rather than calling for the burning of the halls of God, the poem laments the laneways of life in the city Lot's wife loved. This poem does not just critique violence, it also critiques the reading that justifies violence.

The moral coil of this poem is one of power, love and memory. The work exposes violence as violence, no matter how it's dressed up, and invites its readers to bear witness to the stories erased by ideologies. Natalie Diaz demonstrates the necessity of imagination to reinterpret powerful stories. She joins the many poets who take the craft of poetry, and use that craft to break a biblical or mythological story open, recasting it in a new moral light.

By narrating the story of Lot's wife looking back, Diaz is also looking back; and in looking back, she is also looking out: naming, seeing, seeking. The image towards the end of this poem – '[d]ark thighs of smoke opened / to the sky' – makes me see the story of Sodom as a birthing. What is this burning city going to birth in the future? It's like Lot's wife can see how this story of destruction will continue to smoke for centuries. Terror, as the poem tells it, can give birth to terror. So many of the world's stories – in mythologies, sacred texts, cultures – have been used to justify the unjustifiable. Rather than reject this story, Natalie Diaz redeems it.

In a single poem, there can be a marriage between unexpected things: a marriage between the living and the dead; a marriage between hope and brutal reality; a marriage between friendship and the griefs that friendships carry.

Poetry doesn't attempt to resolve these strange arrangements. Poetry doesn't say we have to choose between happiness and sadness, between grief and relief, between catharsis and solitude. Poetry knows that there can always be more than one thing happening at a time.

After the Goose that Rose like the God of Geese

Martín Espada

> *Everything that lives is Holy.*
> —William Blake

After the phone call about my father far away,
after the next-day flight canceled by the blizzard,
after the last words left unsaid between us,
after the harvest of the organs at the morgue,
after the mortuary and cremation of the body,
after the box of ashes shipped to my door by mail,
after the memorial service for him in Brooklyn,

I said: *I want to feed the birds. I want to feed bread*
to the birds. I want to feed bread to the birds at the park.

After the walk around the pond and the war memorial,
after the signs at every step that read, *Do Not Feed the Geese*,
after the goose that rose from the water like the god of geese,
after the goose that shrieked like a demon from the hell of geese,
after the goose that scattered the creatures smaller than geese,
after the hard beak, the wild mouth taking bread from my hand,

there was quiet in my head, no cacophony of the dead
lost in the catacombs, no mosquito hum of condolences,
only the next offering of bread raised up in my open hand,
the bread warm on the table of my truce with the world.

After the sudden death of an old friend, I found myself forgetting everything I'd known about grief. It was at the start of Covid so there was nothing to do: a funeral on Zoom, and that was it. I had ideas about arranging a kind of virtual wake, but that fell flat. I had more time than I'm used to, because the pandemic was young and not everything had gone online. So I knitted. I knitted with frenzy. I'm a mediocre knitter now, but then I was abominable. I put on mindless television and half listened to it while knitting terrible scarves every night. I didn't have much wool, so I'd rip it all apart before going to bed, starting again the next day.

This poem of Martín Espada's is stitched together by a particular word: the word *after.* After what? we might ask. Poetry has a certain kind of music to it, and sometimes that music is built by rhythm, or formal rhyme, or half rhyme, by words beginning with the same letter, or repeated vowel sounds creating an echo. A repeated word at the start of a sentence – the word *after* in this poem – is evidence of a poem's music. This device is known as *anaphora* in poetry, a word meaning 'to carry up'. The repeated *after* in the body of 'After the Goose that Rose like the God of Geese' creates a feeling of rhythm and exhaustion. 'After' is hoping for the *next* thing, which is another way of hoping for *something* to end. And after the after? The quiet, the simplicity of a hand – an open hand – offering bread to a goose, like a truce, or communion. The poem rests, the goose is the god that brought calm to the frenzy of grief. The poem – and the reader – can breathe.

There are different kinds of deaths: expected ones, shocking ones, deaths that come after everything's been said, deaths that come before anything's been said. With 'after the last words left unsaid between us' we hear that death has arrived in the speaker's life. He got a phone call saying his father was dying, and wanted to make it but couldn't – perhaps because of the blizzard – so then certain affirmations, or recriminations, or stories remained unvoiced. Maybe he wished to offer an apology, or dreamed of receiving one. Who knows? This could have been an easy or a difficult relationship. The hospitality of this poem is that even though it's describing his grief, it could also be about yours, or mine. There are many griefs held together in these generous lines.

Beyond the things to do, beyond the congregation and a memorial service, the speaker in the poem wishes for solitude – him and bread and birds in the park. He wants to witness and satisfy another hunger – the unambiguous hunger of a bird – perhaps because that'll help him think of his own unsatisfied grief. In grief, it can be helpful to have something to do.

Feeding the bird, this bird like the 'god of geese' who 'shrieked like a demon from the hell of geese', feels like a feral Eucharist. Espada has taken bread to something wild. The goose is an object of fury, and is selfish, almost, in scattering smaller birds, reaching with its sharp beak, committed to and consumed with its own hunger. If this is a eucharistic poem, it's speaking about a Eucharist that can satisfy all our furies and fires, all our hells and hungers. The goose defies order, defies demure behaviour. The goose doesn't give a damn. It is hungry. It fights to eat. The goose will break the body of a small bird if it needs to.

Everything that lives is Holy is the poem's epigraph – a quote from William Blake's magnificent work *The Marriage of Heaven and Hell*, written in the late 1700s, a book that reads like a kind of scripture, but not any scripture you'd hear in church. This is a scripture for the artist, for the one who has felt raw abandonment. There are proverbs of hell in Blake's book. Martín Espada's poem is about God and a goose being tied together in a screaming frenzy; about grief and desire, about a dead father and a living son. I'm not surprised he needed Blake to remind and reassure him of the holiness of living, and everything it brings.

The poem invites us to pay attention to the strange desires that occur in grief, the tangible things we feel compelled to do – unbidden and unexplained rituals that might bring about a calm within their own strange logic. *Listen*, this poem says, *if you wish to feed the birds, then feed the birds; this, too, is an impulse of survival*. This poem invites us, I think, to engage in rituals of the body, purely physical. Such rituals don't have to symbolise or mean anything – they are their own evidence of living, evidence of things that continue even while we grieve. Strangely, in this poem of thirteen afters, of the mounting pressure in grief, it is in the shrieking and then the calming of a hungry animal that Martín Espada finds what comes after *after*. He is in his body, we see his open hand. The goose is fed, the grieving man is calmed. It is – for now – enough.

I started writing poems when I was eleven. For years, I carried those poems around with me like they were a secret scripture, stashed in my bag, hidden in the backs of books. All those early poems are lost now. But they're in my body – I remember the hunger that drove them, the things that made me need to write them.

My Mother's Body

Marie Howe

Bless my mother's body, the first song of her beating
heart and her breathing, her voice, which I could dimly hear,

grew louder. From inside her body I heard almost every word she said.
Within that girl I drove to the store and back, her feet pressing

the pedals of the blue car, her voice, first gate to the cold sunny
    mornings,
rain, moonlight, snow fall, dogs . . .

Her kidneys failed, the womb where I once lived is gone.
Her young astonished body pushed me down that long corridor,

and my body hurt her, I know that – 24 years old. I'm old enough
to be that girl's mother, to smooth her hair, to look into her exultant
    frightened eyes,

her bedsheets stained with chocolate, her heart in constant failure.
It's a girl, someone must have said. She must have kissed me

with her mouth, first grief, first air,
and soon I was drinking her, first food, I was eating my mother,

slumped in her wheelchair, one of my brothers pushing it,
across the snowy lawn, her eyes fixed, her face averted.

Bless this body she made, my long legs, her long arms and fingers,
our voice in my throat speaking to you now.

If you were to be given a poetry exercise that said: *write a poem where you enter into time through various portals, recalibrating the perspective and point of view of the poem's speaker through the subjectivity of wisdom, desire, need and strength,* you might be bored, or confused, or interested. This brilliant poem is born from Marie Howe's extraordinary poetic intelligence, an intelligence that demonstrates how time can be experienced in multiple ways at once.

The first time I read this poem, I felt like I was in a time warp. Standing in the body of the poem, with only Marie Howe's voice for company, I was able to look backwards and forwards at the same time. With perfect ease, this poem opens up windows in time and invites us to look through: seeing a person when they are born, seeing a person when they die, seeing this person when they are younger than we are now, even though we could never have seen them that way when they were alive.

The poem's opening and closing sentences begin with the word 'bless': 'Bless my mother's body' and 'Bless this body she made'. What is this word *bless*? It's a word of kindness, a word of beatitude, a word of generous enfolding: *Let me wrap you in a word that is meant for pure goodness*. Both the title and the first line refer to 'my mother's body'. By blessing her mother's body, Marie Howe is also blessing the body from which her own body came. Blessing, like time, goes in many directions.

This is a carnal poem; *carnal* coming from the Latin *carne* meaning *meat*. It takes the reality of embodiment seriously. We see the mother's heart, hear her breathing, we are 'inside her body' 'pressing // the pedals of the blue car'. Then time shifts, and we are at the end of the mother's life, where her kidneys fail and her womb is gone. Then we're back again at the moment she gave birth: 'Her young astonished body pushed me down that long corridor, // and my body hurt her'. Love is embodied in the unforgettable line: 'and soon I was drinking her, first food, I was eating my mother'. Then, in the space of a linebreak it is the mother who is being pushed in a wheelchair toward the end of her life. This poem knows the ways love is housed in the changing shape and needs of our bodies – growing, leaving, giving, taking, feeding, pushing.

While 'My Mother's Body' doesn't include the word *forgiveness*, it is nonetheless a poem about forgiveness. Somewhere in the gaps between the words, the poem suggests that it wasn't always easy being this mother's daughter; or this daughter's mother. 'It's a girl, someone must have said. She must have kissed me // with her mouth, first grief, first air.'

The poem isn't accusatory, rather there's a mature voice speaking, a voice that has learned its own lessons in love and disappointment, in parenthood and failure, in pain and promise. Embedded in this poem is the possibility that some complicated family relationships can be eased by taking that long view of time.

While the mother character is the focus of the poem, quietly, the age of the poet is being considered too: she's being born, she's maturing, she's with her mother when the mother is near death. To take this view of time is to see another long corridor: that from birth to death; the deaths of our parents, and of ourselves.

I remember the first time I realised I was old enough to be the parent of an adult I was speaking to. Now, it happens often. I'm used to it, but it took time. As I'm writing this, I'm forty-five. When my mother was forty-five, I was eighteen. And I didn't know how to be an eighteen-year-old, nobody had taught me – I felt alone, and filled with a mixture of melodrama and grief. Now, when I think of my mother at forty-five, I understand that of course she didn't know how to mother the young man I was. I didn't know how to be him. 'My Mother's Body' helps me bless my own mother's body and her life. I see her forty-fifth year in a new way, and through this, I also see myself.

Every poem deserves to be read multiple times. In a second – or third, or fourth – reading of 'My Mother's Body', it becomes clear how often the simple word 'her' is used: her body, her feet, her womb, her bedsheets, her mouth, her wheelchair . . . nineteen times in total. The single-syllable sound of the word 'her' is a thread that holds the poem together. It's like a familiar chord in a song, something that keeps you homed to a particular key. And so it is a piece of poetic brilliance that the final line doesn't include it: 'Our voice in my throat speaking to you now.' It's the only time the word 'our' appears in the poem. Nowhere else. Maybe everybody said that the poet and her mother sounded alike on the telephone. Now the mother is gone, but is living in the voice of the poem, and in the voice of whomever is reading the poem. We hear her now.

Every time I'm on a bus – which is quite often – I have this ridiculous fantasy. 'If this bus were to break down now, what would we all talk about?'

In reality, people would probably get on their phones, look up complaint forms, ask about toilets and make calls to explain they'd be late. In my fantasy however, people turn to each other for conversation. 'What's a before-and-after moment of your life?' we could ask each other. And then we could listen.

Father

Carlos Andrés Gómez

I

In the basement of the crack house   I used to visit
as an outreach worker   on 121st street in Harlem,
I was convinced   He   refused
to travel north of 96th.   I wrote a letter
to Joanna on her mission   in Taiwan, detailed
each irrefutable   piece of evidence   proving
we are all,   in fact,   alone.
Told her about   the nine-year-old orphan
forced   to sell   her body
for three years   before ending up   just off
Times Square,   discarded   in a dumpster.
I told her about   the eldest son
who answered   a burglar's call   and was shot,
paralyzed   from the waist down.   I asked her
about drought   and famine   and endless
civil wars – what lessons   does His book
refuse?

II

When her heart rate   dropped by half   in less
than a minute,   the population   of our cramped
hospital room   tripling   in a handful of seconds,
I grasped for   anything   that would keep me
upright.   At first,   the wall: cool and steady,
demanding my body   ascend beyond   what seemed
possible.   Then,   nothing,
no one.   I stood   in the waiting room
of the O.R.   waiting   to be called in,

to find out if   my child   had survived.
I spent each second   trying to pull tiny shoe-coverings
over my too-large feet.   I confessed   every wrong
of my life   to an empty, overlit room   of steel
and sterile instruments   that all   reflected back
distorted   versions of myself.   I fumbled
for any prayer   I could remember, hoping
that I had all along been   mistaken   about the hollow
blackness   of the infinite sky.   I never wanted
so badly   to have been wrong
about anything   in my life—

                    and then   a   disembodied
                 voice   called out,   seemingly only to me —
                    a tiny growl   at first   that blossomed
              into a wail dwarfing   any thought   my mind
                    could   possibly   hold,   any faith
                    I'd ever been   so foolish   to claim.

I first read Carlos Andrés Gómez's poem 'Father' in a collection titled *Hijito*, meaning 'son'. It's a poem about becoming a father, yes, and it's also a poem about fear, religion, conversion and being a man.

From the opening lines, so much about the poet's own life is narrated: he's a qualified social worker and has interests in questions of religion and justice. He knows how complicated life can be. He turns to his friends when he needs to process: he's dismayed at the circumstances the young people in his care face, and writes of this dismay to his friend Joanna – on mission in Taiwan – daring her to contradict his conclusions. He uses evidence: a trafficked nine-year-old; a boy shot in a robbery; drought; famine; war. He's present to critique, professionalism, faith and friendship.

The heart of this poem, to begin with, is theological: if God is the Father of all, then what is this? If God were father, he'd be powerful, he'd intervene. Then the poem turns: the poet becomes a parent; there's panic in the birthing suite, with a dropped heart-rate – of either the child or mother – and Carlos's first experience of fatherhood is one of profound helplessness. He can do nothing, but he'll try anything– confession and prayer included, doubts be damned. Then the cry of a newborn – 'a tiny growl' – and everything is changed. He walks into fatherhood through the door of weakness, of helplessness, of desperation, of needing help.

Is this a poem about the idea of God? Or about the experience of becoming a parent? For many people, both are linked. The speaker's understanding of the word 'father' changed after becoming one; and that 'all-powerful' became eradicated from his imagination when his own initiation into that role was one of profound helplessness. What I find enormously relieving about this poem is that its end doesn't revisit the earlier scenes. There is no return to derelict houses, imagining God hiding and suffering in the corners.

The poem's form is striking. It's fragmentary, with spaces between words. Some fragmented poetry occurs because most of it is lost – the almost three-thousand-year-old poetry of Sappho, for instance, survives only in parts, apart from one full poem. Other poems are fragmentary by design, including this one. This work of Carlos Andrés Gómez's is a kind of map, and he is trying to find his way: trying to be a good presence as a social worker; trying to figure out how the world can be like this; trying to understand parenthood through his work; trying to reckon with his own fear as a new father; trying to contain the love and joy that electrify him; trying to contain the new fear that terrifies him. No wonder he uses this form of fragments on the page – he's telling us in those gaps that it's difficult to hold it all together. He's right, it is. That's why he doesn't close them up at the end either; they're unresolved, because that's the world.

My friend Andrew is a backslidden Baptist. The older he got the more he – like Carlos – saw no evidence that God acted like a father. But he felt guilty about this too, because he wasn't raising his children in the faith he was raised in. His four-year-old daughter asked him once where Jesus lived. They were driving – she was strapped into a child seat in the back of the car. He looked at her in the rear-view mirror. 'Jesus lives in your heart,' he said, even though he didn't believe it. She looked at him, with incredulity, and said 'No he doesn't.' It was just a little exchange: a man discussing religion with his daughter, but in this small exchange, his relationship to guilt changed. He was proud of his daughter for having the capacity to speak plain truth. The crisis of faith for him wasn't simply a matter of whether he did or didn't believe in God; the crisis was the means by which he grew as a person in relationship to his questions. For Carlos, too, I believe.

Carlos Andrés Gómez holds a complicated line in this poem: how to think about care, and God, and work, and professionalism; how to think about a failed system that continues to fail children who've been failed at school, at home, by history and by policy. His experiences of love and surrender are a shock to him, but there's no pretence that his new role as father will change anything for his clients. Perhaps the only thing that's holding him together is the ability to keep trying. That might explain the gaps in the lines in this poem too: the swollen heart of a new father; the gaps he sees in the environments his clients inhabit, the ways in which they've been failed by a system that should care enough to not fail so spectacularly.

The final word in the poem is 'claim'.

> and then   a   disembodied
> voice   called out,   seemingly only to me –
> a tiny growl   at first   that blossomed
> into a wail dwarfing   any thought   my mind
> could   possibly   hold,   any faith
> I'd ever been   so foolish   to claim.

The word 'claim' contains power, because it is a word of power: to claim is to own; to claim is to dismiss; to claim is to have knowledge over. This new father is realising that he won't be able to claim anything; rather, he'll need to accept, and depend on, help. Power is reframed: suddenly he's less interested in the question as to whether there's a God or not, and whether that God is a good father, instead he's asking what it'll mean for *him* to be a father and how that will influence his work, whether he'll be good enough or not.

After Heath Ledger played the Joker in *The Dark Knight*, a Batman film directed by Christopher Nolan, I remember hearing someone on the radio say that Ledger had elevated that character to the level of theatre: 'Because of Heath Ledger's work, actors in the future will want to offer *their* reinterpretation of the Joker.' Or, at least, that's something like what he said.

He was right: in 2019, Joaquin Phoenix played the titular character in *Joker*, directed by Todd Phillips. Certain characters enter the public imagination and ask to be interpreted and reinterpreted; whether that's a character from religion or fiction, Shakespeare or Austen. The characters keep coming back, because we need them.

Man and Boy

Patience Agbabi

And Abraham stretched forth his hand,
and took the knife to slay his son.
                                        – Genesis 22:10

Open the blind, son. Wide. I'm not dead yet.
Did you hear the hail? Like it was deep frying.
Your mother says forked and sheet lightning
at the same time spells trouble. I know she is.
What's it like, the sky? Blue-grey? Grey-blue?
I wish I could see it too. Like surround
sound with the ghost of a picture.
What's the use? I'm dying. Give me your hand.
Hairy from day one, you were. Born old.
We knew your mother was expecting twins,
expected one of each. Your brother Jacob
followed, gripping your heel, a born tackler.
He takes after your mother. Never trust
a woman. He intends to run the business,
but you were first. There's something I must tell you . . .
I've so few pleasures left. Will you prepare it?
It's OK. Use the Volvo. I'm not going
anywhere, am I? Son, I know you do.

Who is it? Son, is that you? Back so soon?
Come off it. Do you take me for senile?
I've taken leave of one of my senses
not five. Come a bit closer. I don't bite.
You smell, feel like my eldest son yet sound
like Jacob. Is this some kind of a joke?

Forgive me, son. Must be the side effects,
it isn't age that kills you, it's the drugs.
You know there's too much pepper in this soup.
OK. I've kept it buried long enough.
Do something for me first, though. Lock the door
and if your brother knocks, don't answer it.

No one knows this. Not even your mother.
I wish you'd known your grandfather. We're all
cut from the same plain cloth. Identical.
I was an only child, my father and I
did everything together, man and boy.
I'd just turned twelve. My father woke me early,
We're going for a drive. There were two men
I didn't know, the one on the back seat
beside me had black hair, a nervous twitch.
The car smelt of sweat and burning leather.
The journey took forever. No one spoke.
The next thing I remember is the office.
A huge black director's chair, a table,
a telephone, the décor was old-fashioned
but classy. Me, my father, no one else.
Sit down, son. I've never felt so small.
And then he did the thing that shocked me more
than anything that happened since. He tied me.
Tied me to the chair. No. I didn't.
He was my father and his word was law.
He pressed a gun hard up against my head,
my inner eye. Twelve years flashed in a second.
Then the explosion of the phone ringing.
It rang eight times before he answered it.
He didn't speak. Just put down the receiver

and fired the gun toward the candelabra.
We never talked about it. In the car
on the way home, I noticed his grey hairs
for the first time. I never blamed him for it,
I understood. He always kept his word.
He would have fired that shot. He knew I knew.

Bless you son, I'm fine. I need to sleep.
Wake me in three hours' time. I'll drink to that.
Who is it? Who? I'm far too old for this.
If you are who you say you are, then who
the hell sat on my bed, shared my secret?
I've lived too long. He should have pulled the trigger.
Where are my tablets? I'm a dead man.
I have two sons . . . forked and sheet lightning . . .
first come, first served. The sins of the father . . .
Forgive me, son. He let it ring eight times.
I'm sorry, I'm too weak now. Ask your brother.
There's too much salt, I have no appetite.
He went grey overnight. Where are my tablets?
What time is it? Where am I? Who are you?
I only have one son, never had two.

This is a persona poem written in the voice of the Jewish patriarch Isaac. Before getting into the story that's being narrated – which will be familiar to some and unfamiliar to others – it's worthwhile considering the persona poem. A *persona* used to mean a mask, and this is a helpful way to look at this form: it's a mask used by a poet where the mask resembles – or is meant to resemble at least – another character. In this way, Patience Agbabi is able to speak in the first person of a biblical patriarch. She can say 'I'm not dead yet' in the first line of 'Man and Boy' and be heard in the voice of someone who actually is dead. So already we know that there's a piece of theatre happening: the dead character *is* dead. There's tension in the drama of perspectives happening in the 'I'. We're tempted to wonder why this poet wants to make this dead character say these things.

There are many persona poems written from the voice of some Greek god or other, and I regularly have to read up about the story along with the poem in order to better understand how the original story is reinterpreted, retold, taken on as a mask by the particular poet. Fiona Benson's Zeus sequence in *Vertigo & Ghost* had me searching online articles for the various forms that Zeus takes, for instance, and the musical *Hadestown* sent me to the underworld. Not knowing the original story can be a benefit, because the role of a fresh reader is a helpful one for any poem based in myth. I always find it important to notice – and then ignore

– any judgment I feel for not knowing a particular myth. There are too many stories to know them all and the real question is: will the story work its magic on you?

In 'Man and Boy' Patience Agbabi takes on the voice of Isaac, particularly amplifying the tragic nature of his character: Isaac was one of the long-awaited sons of Abraham, a complicated, conflicted man who'd been waiting all his life to be the father of nations. When Isaac was a young man, God tested Abraham by saying: 'Are you willing to sacrifice your son?' It is a traumatic story. Abraham takes Isaac on a long journey up a sacred mountain, ties him up, lifts a knife, and is about to stab him when an angel shouts at him, saying 'Abraham! Abraham!' twice. Have you ever heard an angel panic? This story has. The angel had to repeat Abraham's name in order to interrupt Abraham's frenzy and tell him he'd passed the test.

Isaac doesn't ever recover. He goes down the mountain separately from Abraham, and never sees either his father or mother again. Later in life, married with twin sons, he loses his sight and becomes obsessed with death. His own father had died without passing on a blessing to him, so now Isaac – even though he's nowhere near death – is convinced he needs to pass on his blessing, in order not to let history repeat itself. He has a favourite son: the older twin – hairier, coarser – but his wife prefers the younger one. Isaac sends the older son off to make soup, saying that he'll give his blessing when that son brings the soup back. However, he's tricked. The younger one brings soup first, and deceives his father by wearing a pelt to seem hairy like his brother. The younger son gets the blessing meant for the older. It's a story of deception, sibling rivalry, obsession with death, the way that trauma passes down through generations; and also a story about men, masculinity, fear, rage and power.

Patience Agbabi manages, in only about seven hundred words, to bring us into Isaac's mindset. The short sentences build up a frenetic pace, communicating anxiety. Isaac isn't 'dead yet' but is obsessed with death: he perceives threat in the hail, in the lightning, in the thing that sounds like frying. He is burdened with his story of trauma, he feels a desperate desire to share it, but is also ambivalent about sharing it: why else does he demand that favourite dish if not to delay the telling of what he most wishes to tell? 'I'm not going / anywhere, am I?' Isaac is so frightened of death that he's barely living.

The second and third verses of the poem recount Isaac sharing that awful story with who he thinks is his favourite son, but is actually the younger twin, disguised as the older, wearing his clothes and fur: 'You smell, feel like my eldest son yet sound / like Jacob. Is this some kind of a joke?' Isaac's way of passing his blessing is to share the story of his life – the trauma that unhinged him; the nightmare he remembers, even though he probably wishes he could forget. Agbabi contemporises Isaac's story: there's a car, a gun, a boardroom. Abraham presses the gun up against Isaac's head, and we're all waiting for the BANG, but instead it's a phone, ringing, ringing, ringing . . . over and over, just like that damned angel shouting *Abraham, Abraham.* Abraham shoots the gun towards the candelabra, and on the drive home the boy notices his father's greying hair. Now, years later, a father himself, Isaac hopes that telling this story will help him live, or will help explain his life. Perhaps he's hoping that a burden shared will be a burden lightened.

Whatever his reason for wishing to tell his story, it achieves nothing, because in the final stanza of the poem, Isaac realises he's been deceived. Isaac begins to panic, to repeat himself, to slip back into trauma. His speech becomes fragmentary:

Where are my tablets? I'm a dead man.
I have two sons . . . forked and sheet lightning . . .
first come, first served. The sins of the father . . .

The old man who still feels laden down by the actions of his father, now in pain because of the actions of a son.

This brilliant retelling of this story evokes deep sympathy for the character of Isaac: alone, deceived again, lost, confused, unsure who he is even though he's from a line of the great patriarchs. Interestingly, Patience often writes in male personas, and does so brilliantly, trying on masks of masculinity, or whiteness, or religion. In so doing she reveals and conceals at once.

Why is this a good story? It's tragic, and certainly in the way Patience Agbabi tells it, the character of Isaac is pitiful. Perhaps the world needs stories of how pain can sometimes continue in order to help those of us who also carry pain. As it happens, in the biblical story, the twin brothers eventually reconcile, and they begin to heal their family line. But in this poem there's no easy ending – Patience lets the chaos echo for a while. That's part of the poem's work: to show that art is sometimes comforting when it refuses to comfort, that it can be a good thing to hear an echo of the truth of pain, without rushing headlong into resolution.

Short poems usually take a long time to arrive. For a while – and maybe still – the shortest poem in the English language was one written by the actor and politician Gyles Brandreth. It's titled 'Ode to a Goldfish' and it contains three words:

O
Wet
Pet

I heard him recite it during an interview when I was a teenager. It's the easiest poem I know to learn off by heart.

On Receiving Father at JFK after his Long Flight from Kashmir

Rafiq Kathwari

As I fling my arms wide, he extends his hand.

This is an extraordinary poem. With a title of eleven words and the full, one-lined body of the poem consisting only of ten, it's easily remembered and endlessly explorable. I first read this poem when Rafiq Kathwari's book *In Another Country* won the Patrick Kavanagh Award in Ireland in 2013, and it's a poem to which I continue to return. In 2020, with social distancing and anxiety about touch becoming widespread due to Covid, the poem took on new echoes.

Rafiq Kathwari is a poet from Kashmir, that territory disputed between Pakistan and India. He grew up there, and as a young man moved to New York. In middle age, he moved to Ireland, and now divides his time between those three places: Ireland, New York and Kashmir. His poetry explores some of the great themes of literature: family, pain, politics, separation, borders, distance, love.

The tension between the title and the body of this poem is striking, and perhaps all the more so because of its brevity. There's a strange kind of formality to the title: the older man is not 'Dad' or even 'My Father' but instead 'Father'. This father character isn't *welcomed* or *met*; neither is the son *picking up my father at the airport*. He's being received – again, there's a formality to the word choice. The formality is undone by the image of a son flinging his arms, and not just flinging them, but flinging them wide. Then the formality returns: an extended hand for a handshake.

I've read this poem with many groups, and there are always strong reactions to it. Some people imagine the father to be emotionally incompetent. Others say: *That's just like my family*, or speak about generational or cultural gaps. The brilliance of this poem is that it doesn't interpret itself; and the blank space of the page – all of that emptiness – invites the projections of the reader. Using this form, Rafiq Kathwari makes space for all the things he is not saying, as well as all the things a reader might want to make the poem say. All we know is that a son got ready for a hug; a father went for a handshake.

Some read this poem as a depiction of culturally conditioned awkwardness between two men. This might be an accurate reading, or not. A Greek friend of mine kisses his father every time he greets him; an Australian friend told me that he never feels more loved than when he hugs his dad; an Indian friend often holds my hand when we meet. Not every culture discourages affection between men; many cultures expect it.

Perhaps the father was very affectionate yet anxious about affection in public places. *I'll hug you when we're at home*. The title tells us that the father's just gotten off the 'Long Flight from Kashmir' – maybe he's conscious of it having been many hours since he's washed, and he's feeling uncomfortable. Maybe the father is affectionate with some people but not his son. Maybe this is the first time the son has flung his arms out like this and the father did not want to make assumptions. Maybe he is uptight. The list is endless – and even though Kathwari could put us all right by telling us what the particularities between the son and father are, the poem allows for the space where we become the child, or the parent; where we are in the gap between affection and restraint; where we can make the reasons as plural as we need. The blank space of this poem shares a story of particularity, allowing – by restraint – for it to hold multitudes.

A poem like this takes on a new layer of meaning when read in the aftermath of Covid, even though it was published long before then. It could be summarised as a younger person wishing to show affection to a parent in public. Hugging, kissing, even handshakes were all forbidden during the height of the pandemic. In a time where millions of people have been mindful to avoid even careful touch with someone they love, a poem describing two different modes of greeting has new meanings. Time works its own strangeness on the reading of a poem.

As well as being a poet, Rafiq Kathwari is also a translator, and has worked on translating the Urdu poetry of Sir Muhammed Iqbal. He's written widely about mental health – his own mother lived with schizophrenia – and particularly about mental health in Kashmir during the Covid pandemic. In this way, ideas of family, affection, struggle, and partition are all underlying themes of his work. It's possible, perhaps, to see some of these elements in the poem, too: the space between a father and a son (perhaps the gap of generations), together with the absence of his mother in the poem and the way that affection is transmitted by the body in different languages depending on which man you're looking at.

My formal training in literature began by reading the Bible. For years, I was in an environment of fear where all such literature had to be interpreted through one anxious question: what is the singular meaning of this text? As years went by – and as I got better teachers – I began to learn that a good text might have five or six interesting meanings. I realised that good literature lasts, not because it has one interpretation, but because successive generations of readers have given it careful attention; using their understanding, learning, imagination and lives. This kind of reading allows language to breathe, to be part of an evolving exchange. Rafiq Kathwari's ten-word poem is an extraordinary demonstration of his trust in language, and in the space around language that's filled with many possible understandings. This is a poem that looks back as it's looked at. What does it see?

If a poem's like a house, then the house probably has many different entry points: a window, a door, a crack in the walls. Hell, you can probably burrow through the foundations and push up through the floor. A poem can offer dozens of entryways, opening then to many meanings.

Essay on Reentry

Reginald Dwayne Betts

At two a.m., without enough spirits
spilling into my liver to know
to keep my mouth shut, my youngest
learned of years I spent inside a box: a spell,
a kind of incantation I was under; not whisky,
but History: I robbed a man. This, months
before he would drop bucket after bucket
on opposing players, the entire bedraggled
bunch five & six & he leaping as if
every lay-up erases something. That's how
I saw it, my screaming-coaching-sweating
presence recompense for the pen. My father
has never seen me play ball is part of this.
My oldest knew, told of my crimes by
a stranger. Tell me we aren't running
towards failure is what I want to ask my sons,
but it is two in the a.m. The oldest has gone off
to dream in the comfort of his room, the youngest
despite him seeming more lucid than me,
just reflects cartoons back from his eyes.
So when he tells me, Daddy it's okay, I know
what's happening is some straggling angel,
lost from his pack finding a way to fulfil his
duty, lending words to this kid who crawls
into my arms, wanting, more than stories
of my prison, the sleep that he fought while
I held court at a bar with men who knew
that when the drinking was done,
the drinking wouldn't make the stories
we brought home any easier to tell.

I googled 'what is a man?' and the answers came in from religion, psychology, fashion, science, linguistics, queer studies and philosophy. This poem by Reginald Dwayne Betts considers what it is to be a man through the lens of a conversation between a father and son in the middle of the night. 'Essay on Reentry' explores what it means to be *this* man, awake late, the television on but turned down, his younger son sitting next to him, eyes mirroring the images on the screen. We're with the speaker in this room – this solid stanza of a poem – and it is dark, he has something to say, and he's wondering whether there's ever a good time to say it.

Identity is a theme here: the speaker is about to introduce a different self to his son. He has many identities: he's a man with friends, a father, a son, a man interested in sports and coaching, a man awake at night. None of these are too complicated: either for the father or the son. But *felon* is an identity put upon the father, and *son of a felon* soon will be for the son. Who decides the hierarchy of selves? What's happening in this night-time scene isn't just a private family story, it's a societal one too. The son will have to learn to live with the social impact of what he hears that night. In this way, time is a theme in this poem too: not just because it's two a.m., but because time was served, and though that time is finished, it continues to come knocking on the life of the speaker and his family, even years after everything is done.

This is a scene-led narrative poem, a poem that tells a story. It starts at two a.m.; then some of the father's story is told; then the scene flips to a father coaching his son playing basketball; then we learn of the father's absent father; then we're back at two a.m. The scenes progress in time, but flash back, before returning to the poem's central action.

A simplicity of language, lack of artifice and raw vulnerability are all present. As a reader, you're left wondering how the father felt when his older son heard stories about him from a stranger; we see – or hear – the father as 'screaming-coaching-sweating' coach; and we can understand the desperate attempt to repay absence with presence. Even though the father's father is not present in the poem, the implication of his absence is. Reginald Dwayne Betts has crafted a poem where loss threatens to repeat itself. The poem's title – 'Essay on Reentry' – is not just referring to the day of coming home from having served a sentence, but the complications and complexities it implies for the future.

When Reginald Dwayne Betts was sixteen, he was sentenced to an eight-year prison sentence – fourteen months of which he spent in solitary confinement – for a carjacking. While in solitary, somebody – he never knew who – put books through his door, including, at one point, the 1971 poetry anthology *The Black Poets*. Betts describes this as his doorway into poetry. When he left prison, he went to the University of Maryland, and then on to study law. Now he's completed a PhD in Law at Yale. His poetry collection *Felon* queries time and race in America, and many of the poems, including this one, put certain terms under the spotlight: 'inside a box', for instance, and 'spell'; 'recompense', 'pen' and 'I held court.'

'Essay on Reentry' depicts men reaching out: the father reaches out to his friends during evenings at a bar; he reaches out to the son awake in the middle of the night, while lamenting his own boyhood's lack of such connection; his evenings at the bar could be seen as another attempt to reach himself too. In many ways, the poem explores masculinities and the ways that males can be connected – or distanced – by vulnerability and sadness and pain. In the face of those, the father does what he knows he must, all the while worrying how his young son will cope when he hears this story of his father's past. But the worry is displaced by surprise: the son calls him 'Daddy'. In revealing one identity, a deeper one is cherished, and in that light, the son too is seen anew: like an angel 'lost from his pack'. The father sees the son in a new light, because his son saw an old light in him.

While this poem is an extraordinarily intimate portrait of a family at night – of the anxieties a father holds for his sons, and of how a particular story follows him around – this poem also looks out, using the lens of a single story to critique a system whereby individuals are still serving time long after they have served their time. Briefly answering curiosities a reader might have – and god, I wish it were otherwise – Reginald Dwayne Betts allows this poem to look back at the reader and ask questions of its own: does a reentry that must continually reoccur serve any kind of purpose?

A poem can mean different things to you at different stages of your life. When I was a child, I loved Seán Ó Ríordáin's Irish-language poem 'Oíche Nollaig na mBan'. It's a poem about a midlife crisis, but when I was young, I loved the drama of the language, and sound of a storm in the poem. In midlife now, I read that poem most years in January, and it's the crisis of quiet I hear in it. Poems age with their readers.

Married Love

Kathleen Flenniken

All of them are dead now.
My father and mother, bedded together

under their matching stones.
Their married friends, close by.

The crystal and good plates all washed
and put away in other homes,

no party food left over. My job
was to whip the cream for dessert

and ride behind on their fishing weekends
like a seventh wheel,

along with our Airedale who wore
striped socks over his muddy paws

in the house. Spirits accelerated
towards cocktail hour in the red

ranch kitchen where they made
big to-dos over their drinks –

then feigned concern they might
corrupt me. The men stirred

the air, clustered at the bar, moved
among the women conferring

over the bubbling stew.
My mother, flushed and pretty

as a cornucopia of summer fruit.
That September before college

I joined the happy group
on a fly-fishing river in Montana

and slept on the cottage's foldout couch.
Late one evening, lights doused,

I was alone with Mother and one
of the men, not quite uncle

not quite friend though I newly
recognized that he was handsome.

I've erased whatever he said
that convinced me he'd forgotten

I was there. But there I was, afraid
to breathe, confused to learn

how delicately balanced
these practitioners of marriage must be.

Then they retired to their separate rooms,
though a presence hung in the air

like perfume.

I heard Kathleen Flenniken reading a few years ago, at the Unamuno Poetry Festival in Madrid. We all crowded into a magnificent – and tiny – bookshop, Desperate Literature. My memory of hearing Kathleen read is that despite the heat, and the crowd of sixty in a bookshop meant for half that, her poems opened up space. Since coming back from the festival and reading more of her work, I've realised this spaciousness is characteristic of her art. She uses space for observation, reflection, moral reckoning, wist, yearning, and strangeness. This poem 'Married Love' is a perfect example of her poetry.

'Married Love' begins as if it's going to be an elegy to the speaker's parents. Now dead, they lie under matching headstones. These opening lines make me think of pairs of matching pillows on a marital bed; of crockery that matches the tablecloth. This observation comes along with a certain distance, though: her parents' lives are filled with friends, hers seems to be solitary. What a gift to have friends; what a gift to have parents with friends; and, perhaps, what a complication too. All dead now, buried in the earth – their possessions in other homes for other parties.

A deft turn takes place in the fourth couplet: 'no party food left over. My job / was to whip the cream for dessert'. We've gone from imagining where the belongings of dead people are to being in a room where a teenage daughter helps prepare for a party. She's part of the party, but not central to it. She rides 'behind on their fishing weekends / like a seventh wheel'. I see three sets of friends, one of which bring their daughter. Who needs a seventh wheel? The floors in the house are kept clear of the evidence of dog; clear of the evidence of daughter, too? It's a tender poem, without sentimentality. The speaker is present, but not eminent, in her recollection of her parents' attentions.

I remember the strange feeling of beginning to see grown-ups as people not just grown-ups. I realised that they had anxieties, and that they performed their anxieties, sometimes, in the way they interacted with me. In this poem, the adults become aware of the young poet's presence. She's not a girl anymore; not an adult yet either. The adults' pretend concern about cocktails demonstrate their own concerns: about alcohol, about revelry, about what she can see in them.

This poem's careful observations are mostly devoid of judgment, so it's possible to feel both pathos and respect for the speaking voice in the poem all at once. Hers is a childhood filled with parties, trips away, bringing out the crystal and good plates; washing the crystal and good plates, putting them away; following along in the trail of your parents; learning to take jokes from their friends; watching the politics of adults. The speaking voice in 'Married Love' is like the presence described in the final line of the poem: there, like perfume, easy to sense, hard to grasp.

Late one night, waiting for the room to clear of adults so she can make her bed on the couch (again, she's not given a room) Kathleen Flenniken senses the attraction between her mother and another man – a man she, also, recognises as handsome. This is not an affair, but it is the energy of sex in the air. It can be a difficult thing to reckon with your parents' sex life, never mind the desire between one parent and someone else.

What makes the poem more compelling is that we don't know what the mother is thinking, or feeling. She knows her daughter is a witness to this most adult of scenarios. The poem conveys what it means to bear witness to your own appeal: how not be afraid of sex; how not to be controlled by it, either. The speaker's mother is free – in attraction and choice – but the particulars of her life are not narrated.

There are so many possibilities for interpreting this poem. Someone who was lonely might connect with it in one way; someone who was betrayed might connect with it in another; someone might find themselves reflecting on their friendships; and someone might remember when they felt more attractive. Tension and restraint characterises this work: the modest lines, unusual linebreaks and the absence of judgement all suggest, but do not conclude. 'Married Love' is in *conversation* with its readers, asking them to distinguish between the content of the poem, and their associations with it.

There are no strict rhyming patterns here, but there are small echoes of rhyme throughout: 'dead' / 'bedded'; the repeated 'O' sounds – like music, or pleasure – in 'stones', 'close', 'homes', 'over'. I'll leave you to wonder about 'whipping the cream', but 'cream' receives an echo in 'weekends' and 'wheel'. After a gap of rhyme, it picks up again with 'moved' and 'stew' and 'fruit' and 'group'. Then 'doused' and 'couch' make us think of an approaching night. 'Men' and 'friend' rhyme, and in this rhyme we can see the multiple ways rhyme does its work. It establishes music, but also association. The man is 'not quite uncle

// not quite friend' but the rhyme is almost echoing the unconscious: friends, men. Will this teenager make friends of men as she goes to college? Her questions about her own life lurk underneath her observations of her parents' well-populated one.

Kathleen Flenniken is in control of the tempo as the poem closes – I almost imagine whispering the final stanzas. In the end, we're left with a young woman, the summer before college, alone on the fold-out couch after the adults have 'retired to their separate rooms'. They've left a presence, like perfume, behind them. What happened? What did the daughter take from all of this? The poem leaves questions in its wake.

When I was eight or nine, I begged my parents for a copy of the Bible as a Christmas present. They got me a paperback edition for children, with pictures. The first thing I did was to leaf through the pages, searching for a picture of the devil. There he was: sky-blue, with flames for eyes, the hooves of a goat and a pointed tail. I have that Bible still. It never occurred to me then to wonder why *that* was the first thing I looked for: childish fascination with the macabre perhaps. Older now, I have started to wonder.

Exorcism / Freeport

Richard Georges

when I was eight, a priest came and flicked holy water
into the four corners of the wooden house

that kept my parents, two sons, a daughter,
and a darkening forest, in its mouth.

The priest muttered in Latin, crossed us all
with odorous oils, his thumb pausing

at the bottom of each cross, on the small
space of our foreheads where Christ hung –

but the spirits came every night until
my father opened the fowl's throat like a bible,

the glint of metal awash with blood,
a beating of black and white and red feathers.

His hands, the knife, performed their own recital,
to feed with one hand, with the other, kill.

I came across this poem by Richard Georges when I googled 'exorcism' and 'poetry.' That search led me to the *Cordite Review*, where 'Exorcism / Freeport' was initially published. This poem, a sonnet, has all the markings of formality: fourteen lines, a strict rhyming sequence – ab/ab/cd/cd/ee/fg/ hh – and the sonnet's piece of magic, a *volta*: that little turn that indicates a shift, or surprise. Sometimes a poem's volta is a move towards resolution, other times it's a new point of view, or even an uncovering of something unsettling. The volta in this sonnet is placed at the ninth line, making the poem perhaps a little echo of sonnets from Italy. An Italian-echoed sonnet with a priest muttering Latin from a Catholicism that centres its power in Rome.

There are characters in this poem: firstly the narrator, whether this is Richard Georges or not, who tells readers that he was eight, making this a poem of reminiscence, of memory, of awe, too – then the priest; then the rest of the family constellation is mentioned: parents, two sons, a daughter. There's the character of the whatever-it-is-that-needs-to-be-exorcised. Who, or what, is this unnamed thing? It's hard to know, because the poem doesn't show it, preferring to describe its threat than its appearance: a malevolence in a wooden home, with 'a darkening forest, in its mouth.'

Richard Georges is a poet from the British Virgin Islands, although he spent part of his childhood in Trinidad, hence the Freeport of the title. The British Virgin Islands are a collection of over fifty islands just to the east of Puerto Rico. Most of the population lives on the main island, Tortola. The islands were named Santa Úrsula y las Once Mil Vírgenes by Christopher Columbus: Saint Ursula and the Eleven Thousand Virgins. While the islands have been populated for thousands of years, in recent centuries various European powers – the Dutch, Spanish, Danish and English, among others – have made claims of territorial sovereignty.

In 'Exorcism / Freeport' the priest – with his Latin, his oil, his signs of the cross on the foreheads of the family – fails to perform an exorcism: 'the spirits came every night'. In a way, this is not just a failure of the priest, but a failure of the cross, a failure of religion. Whatever power the Catholic religion might have is not able to exert influence. After the turn in the poem, the parent and the priest seem pitted against each other in terms of authority, perhaps alerting us to some of the poem's underlying intuition: empire is unwelcome; local power is what's needed. Perhaps the clash of priest and parent – Father and father – is a way of repre-senting the tension between community tradition and colonising religion.

However, that's only one possibility. It could also be that there is no clash between the two men. This poem can equally present a synchronous approach. There are spirits? Try the sign of the cross. If that doesn't work, try the blood of the fowl. Perhaps this is a poem highlighting how tradi-tions sit side by side.

The father in the poem opens the throat of a fowl 'like a bible'. Even the body of this bird has ritual significance. Richard Georges brings old practices – the smearing of blood taken from a living but dying animal – to the readers through this poem. The glint of the knife, the chaos of the bird's wings, the recital of such brutality, the extinguishing of a bird's life in order to protect human life: this is a practice found in countries the world over. It might bring distaste to many, now, but the echo of this – 'to feed with one hand, with the other, kill' – locates humans among other carnivorous animals. Even our rituals tell that story. Perhaps the father in the poem is a priest too, enacting protection; death and nurture in the one bird's carcass. Richard is not afraid to show us what he, or his speaker, remembers. Perhaps even he does not find this ritual to his liking, but his opinion is not the stuff from which he's making art. His memory is, and the power of that experience from when the speaker was eight.

When I was eighteen, I underwent three exorcisms, the aims of which were to hunt the gay demons from me. It was an invasion of such indignity and embarrassment and fear that it became a fixed point of shame in my life. When I came across this poem by Richard Georges, then, I felt a connection that went far beyond the work that he's exploring in his poem. Perhaps that's one of the functions of art, to become something it could never have been in only the mind of the writer. Richard Georges's sonnet is part of my own armoury now. He never could have known it. Wherever art comes from, it's always bigger than its source.

For years I had a recurring dream. The dream always involved me standing at the mouth of a large cave, knowing I needed to enter, but being undone by fear of what lay inside. I'd wake, petrified. I could describe the whole dream in a second, but when the dream was alive, it felt like time stretched out for eternity – the moment before entering that awful cave would go on forever.

There were all kinds of things alive in me that I wished to be dead in me. I thought the solution would be to cease having those dreams. The dreams had other ideas.

22: La Bota

Esteban Rodríguez

At home, there was nothing your father
couldn't turn his work boots into –
a hammer for loose nails, a prop to even
stubborn tables and chairs, a weapon
to end the lives of anonymous insects.
And there were nights when he would sleepwalk,
and out in the yard with nothing but underwear
on, he'd smack together the bottoms of his boots,
as if there were spirits he had to ward off,
as if his past had taken on some once human form,
and to remind him that no one is ever free
of sin, made it its duty to stalk him at home.
And though it lasted no more than a few minutes,
and your mother would wake him up,
bring him back in, you figured that the boots
had done their job, that the reason he never used
sticks, pots or pans, or yelled at the top
of his lungs was because he wanted the spirit
to know exactly who he was,
that he had every right to be at peace
on whatever ground he walked.

'22: La Bota' is part of a fifty-four-poem sequence titled 'Lotería' by Esteban Rodríguez. Lotería is a Mexican game using fifty-four cards played out in a game of chance that might resemble Bingo. Each card has a number and an image: the first card is El Gallo (the Rooster) and the next card is El Diablito (the Little Devil). The twenty-second card is La Bota, the Boot. Rodríguez uses each image, in this sequence of poems, to open up a window of experience, shock or joy; sometimes from his own life, other times from observation.

The word *objectification* is often heard as a negative word: something forced upon a person. Someone might be objectified for their gender or culture or age – or any one of many parts of their life – frozen in a static view by a speaker who wishes to use them as a prop for a diminishing point or story they wish to tell. Curiously, the verb *to object* calls to mind the original Latin meaning of the word: to put something in the way of. If someone objects to something I'm doing, they are putting something in the way of me continuing to do it. But the word objectification has another use too: in poetry, when an *object* is focused upon, the poem can be understood to use *objectification* as a technique. The object can open up meaning, or mystery. The object is returned to repeatedly, working like a kind of echo, appearing and disappearing throughout the poem.

The objects in this poem – those two boots – are multi-purpose. They first appear as the handyman's tool about the house, functioning as a hammer, or something to steady tables, or 'a weapon / to end the lives of anonymous insects.' Quietly, the poem introduces us to a father: a man whose work requires boots, who takes them off when home. What's his work? Something that requires him to protect his feet. Whether fixing a table or a loose nail, or ridding the house of an insect, he uses his boots to increase ease and safety and comfort. They preside over small matters of life and death, and are a way in which the father joins pride of work with pride of home: what he does outside is fit for inside too.

Then, the turn of the poem, the other side of the card perhaps: the father is asleep, but sleepwalking outside, dressed only in his underwear, carrying his boots and smacking them together 'as if there were spirits he had to ward off' or 'as if his past had taken on some once human form'. The man is no longer a working man, but a haunted man, exposed, barely covered, trying to use noise, or magic, or some kind of territory-marking behaviour to protect himself from spirits. What would those spirits say to him? That he's no good? That he might end? That his past will undo everything he's built? While the boots are the object in the poem, the subject is everything the father's carrying; his past, his dignity, his pride, his protective nature. He's in control of these features in his waking hours, but in his sleepwalking body, they're in control of him.

A friend of mine once had a dream about dismantling his stereo. When he woke, he noticed his stereo neatly dismantled on the desk next to his bed: the screws placed next to each other, the components of his radio laid out neatly, as if for a demonstration, or a dissection. What order had his dreams been concerned with? Dreams reveal so much, while nonetheless being strange outworkings of the unconscious.

In Esteban Rodríguez's poem, the spirits visit the father in his dreams. Why his dreams? Perhaps because that's when he's most vulnerable, with the least amount of protection, even though he has everything to protect.

Of all the defences the father could choose, he doesn't choose pots and pans (which would make a greater noise) or a stick (which could be used as a weapon), but instead turns to those boots. Boots tell his story, they make a thud, and they remind everyone – the living and the dead, even the sleeping man – that he has 'every right to be at peace / on whatever ground he walked.' In this action, there is so much information: are his dreams haunted by voices saying he shouldn't be at peace in the place he lives? The underworld of this poem has echoes of disquiet and displacement, requiring the father to stake his claim to peace and place. Esteban Rodríguez was raised along the Texas–Mexico border. Reading the poem, I wonder if his father's dreams were, perhaps, addressing discriminatory threats against Mexican–Americans, using those boots to establish peace, pride, place and home.

The father and his boots are so strongly emphasised in this poem that it's easy to forget about the speaker. 'At home,' this poem begins, and there's a character speaking, describing parents. What age is the watching son of this poem? I always imagine twelve, although I can't figure out why. Rodríguez keeps a little distance in this poem. He doesn't say 'At home, there was nothing *my* father / couldn't turn his work boots into'. He uses *your* as if he, too, is at a little distance from himself. He and his parents all with their own mysteries and strangeness to confront. Alongside his father's complexities he sees his mother's familiarity with his father's dreamworld troubles; a doorway into the private lives of his parents. We can be so close to each other and yet never fully understand each other; this poem knows this, and is not frightened by it.

If I'm ever editing a poem – of mine, or someone else's – I start by stripping out words. All the adjectives go, and the adverbs. Then any section where the poem's telling me what to feel . . . they go too. I want to see the structure of the poem, to know what its intelligence is, to know its hunger. Only then, seeing its bones, can I know what needs to go back in. Sometimes it's nothing: a poem can tell you many things by showing you only a few.

In Leticia's Kitchen Drawer

Peggy Robles-Alvarado

A Craftsman curved claw hammer to crack coco and
hang
portraits, a tape measure to remind her waist she eats
mangú too often, fifteen scattered rusty pennies to
help Tito with math homework or sink into a nine day
candle to cut Doña Elsa's evil eye on any given day,
five slightly bent nails pulled from the living room wall
that held portraits proving they danced merengue
once, a red silk ribbon to tie his picture to her sweaty
discount store underwear to keep him from falling back
into Tanya's bed, wrinkled menus from the Goodie-
Goodie
Thai restaurant on Cruger she treats herself to when
her sister mocks her for never getting a passport or
mispronouncing Pinot Noir, or not having any Sears
family portraits, a ball of white yarn to wrap around
pasteles every Christmas or to secure lucky leaves above
the doorway when he drinks both their paychecks, film
from
an outdated Kodak she won't develop to avoid seeing
the
exact day she lost her looks on his knuckles, ginger
candy
from the Korean market she reluctantly pushes in her
mouth every time he dares her to leave, every time her
tongue lashes a familiar whip to her body, and when
her voice mimics her sister's burn, Diamond long stick
matches for lighting the broken pilot light and the
candles that keep her bowing to him.

Years ago, a friend said to me that it's often very easy to find the convenience drawer in a kitchen. I've thought about that comment often since then – house-sitting; checking into an Airbnb; visiting someone's house for a wake, or a party. A kitchen drawer is like a story trove: alongside the conveniently reachable everyday items are things of true sentiment: mementoes, objects that hold a story, or tell it back to you.

This poem by Peggy Robles-Alvarado – about a fictional but nonetheless true character named Leticia – is a list of what's found in someone's kitchen drawer. Eleven things: a hammer; a tape measure; pennies; nails; ribbon; a menu; a ball of yarn; undeveloped film; candy; long-stick matches; candles. Each item has a story attached to it, or a threat, a promise, a devotion or a danger. There are sharp things in the drawer as well as string; there are little lights by which to see, or burn, or both.

Many of the items in the drawer are associated with a person in Leticia's life. It's one thing to make your way into a framed photograph in someone's house; it's another thing to have space in someone's drawer of convenience; easy to reach, no luxury, close as skin on skin. We are introduced to Tito, whose homework is aided by fifteen rusty pennies; and we're introduced to Doña Elsa and her evil eye. We hear of people who danced merengue, whose portraits were once on the wall. We hear of a man, presumably a partner, who has made his way to Tanya's bed. Thus we hear of Tanya too. There's the restaurant menu whose food brings comfort to Leticia, and we hear of Leticia's sister, who sometimes brings shame. There are Christmas treats – pasteles – and once again, the 'him' appears: with violence and alcohol and dares. Leticia turns her whipcrack of a tongue on herself, and then we're back to 'him', whoever he is.

Leticia's story is shared through her relationships with objects: she eats coconuts, had portraits, eats mangú. She keeps things – like those rusty pennies. Even though she doesn't want the photos that show her dancing merengue on the living room wall anymore, she keeps the nails. I wonder where the photos went. An item can mean so much more than what it seems: and we hold on to things for so many more reasons than pure sentimentality.

Leticia trusts – or at least tries – rituals: there's a nine-day candle; then after 'he' had gone to the bed of Tanya, she tied a photo of him to her underwear with red silk ribbon. This man doesn't 'go' to Tanya's bed, nor does he 'take' someone; instead Peggy Robles-Alvarado employs the verb 'falling'. What is that falling? Like Adam and Eve falling into temptation based on the advice of a serpent with bad ideas? Leticia inhabits a world that gives permissive verbs to the man's behaviour; verbs she pays the cost of. She wraps yarn around lucky leaves above the doorway: another prayer, another hope, another desperate attempt to make safe what clearly isn't safe. The ginger candy is marketed by some companies as a 'sweet treat that will ease what ails' – anything for comfort. The matches: 'for lighting the broken pilot light and the / candles that keep her bowing to him.' Who is the man she bows to? A god? A devil? It sounds like he thinks he's one but acts like the other.

Leticia feels shamed by her sister: for not being cosmo-politan enough; for mispronouncing the name of a bottle of wine; for not having a passport. A passport is a way out – or at least the dream of a way out. Leticia knows what it's like to be observed: by Doña Elsa's evil eye, by her sister; perhaps implied too is the triumphant gaze of Tanya, into whose bed the man of the poem has fallen. Leticia doesn't have Sears family photos. Her life is one lived under the weight and judgment of other people's gazes, and the drawer is a box of tricks and defences. And when they don't work, she seeks some comfort: food in the Thai restaurant, or mangú, a gorgeous Dominican dish.

Leticia wasn't given the choice to leave the kitchen, a place of domestic kindness, domestic servitude, domestic violence. It's where she lights a candle that keeps her bowing, and the place from which she tries to keep the evil eye at bay. She's got things in the drawer that can hold a life together: a few coins, some ribbon, some yarn, a tape measure. Something to remind her of accusations of the past, of past beauty, and of past beauty taken.

The drawer is an archive of power and powerlessness. It reveals her love, the abuse she suffers, her generosity and devotion, the way she can turn pain in on herself with a sharp tongue. In poetry, there's often *tension*. Sometimes the tension's in the difference between a title and the poem. Sometimes tension's seen in how the lines hold language of dignity and desperation in a very few words. In 'In Leticia's Kitchen Drawer' tension is seen in its powerful restraint, the portrayal of Leticia as a woman caught in a story filled with love and violence. In the poem there are things that could be used as weapons – a curved claw hammer, the evil eye, nails, burning matches – but the person we'd wish to be empowered seems to have the least capacity to use those weapons. To read the poem is to feel the poem's tension and hurt. The tension of the poem isn't just on the page, it's in the bodies and hearts of its readers.

While Yeats, Kavanagh, Nuala Ní Dhomhnaill and Máire Mhac an tSaoi were part of the formal school curricula of my teenage years, it was song lyrics I really turned to for meaning. I knew all the words to all the songs on the few albums I owned. I was the kind of teenager who read the lyrics to the new album on the bus home from the city. And then, as I played the album for the first time, I'd read along again. I'd learn the names of the musicians and producers, and if there was a note from the artist in the liner notes I felt like I'd got my money's worth. If there were no lyrics in the liner notes (hello REM) I felt cheated, but not defeated – I made my own, complete with chord sheets.

I had so much time.

When We Were 13, Jeff's Father Left the Needle Down on a Journey Record Before Leaving the House One Morning and Never Coming Back

Hanif Abdurraqib

and this is why none of us sing along to 'Don't Stop Believin'' when we are being driven by Jeff's mom, four boys packed in the backseat tight like the tobacco in them cigarettes Jeff's mom got riding

shotgun with us around I-270 in a powder blue Ford Taurus where four years later Jeff will lose his virginity to a girl behind the East High School football field then later that night his keys and pants in the school pool so that he has to run

home crying to his mother with an oversized shirt and no pants, like a cartoon bear, and the next day when I hear this story, I will think about what it means for someone to become naked two times in one night to rush into the warmth of two

women, once becoming a man and once becoming a boy all over again but right now it is just us in this car with Jeff's mother, that cigarette smoke dancing from her lips until it catches the breeze

from the cracked front window and glides back towards us a vaga-bond, searching for a throat to move into and cripple while Neal Schon's guitar rides out the speakers and I don't know how many open windows a man has to climb out of in the middle of the night in order to have hands that can make anything scream like that.

nothing knows the sound of abandonment like a highway does, not even God.

in the 1980s, everyone wrote songs about someone leaving except
for this one cuz it's about how the morning explodes over two
people in one bed who didn't know each other the night before
when alone

was the only other option and their homes had too many mirrors
for all that shit and so it is possible that this is the only song
written in the 1980s about how fear turns into promise

I think I know this because there is so much piano spilling

all over our laps that we can't help but to smile since we still
black and know nothing can ransack sorrow like a piano.

Jeff's mother's hand trembles and still wears a wedding ring so
she pulls over to the side of the highway and turns the volume
up so loud after the second guitar solo when the keys kick in
again that we can barely hear the cocktail

of laughter and crying consuming the front seat until the song fades
away and the radio is low again and the ring once on Jeff's mother's
hand is on the side of the highway beneath us, a sacrifice

and so maybe this is why grandma said a piano can coax even
the most vicious of ghosts out of a body.

and so maybe this is why my father would stare at the empty
spaces my mother once occupied, sit me down at a baby grand
and whisper *play me something, child*.

This poem of music and magnificence by Hanif Abdurraqib comes complete with its own soundtrack. From the first time I read this poem, I began humming Journey's 1980s song 'Don't Stop Believin''. I looked up a live performance of it too, and two things remain with me: a) how good they are, and b) the tightness of their jeans.

This is not a poem that leaves a lot of room on the page: it's broad and generous, taking up all the space it needs. Reading the poem, you can hear the contours of everyday speech: somebody is telling a story, then interrupting their own story with another story, then making a reference to music, then back to the story, then slipping in their own grief right at the end. Hanif Abdurraqib is the youngest in a family of four, and he often speaks about there being a lot of talk in his family. Households with lots of people require the skill of interrupting, sometimes even interrupting yourself. You can hear this skill in his poem.

To name some of the characters in this poem is a joyful exercise. There's the speaker, possibly Hanif, as a thirteen-year-old, and Jeff, of course, and Jeff's mother. There are other boys in the back of the car too. There's mention of the girl Jeff was with; and the speaker's own father, and grand-mother. There's the band Journey, especially Neal Schon and his screaming guitar. Some characters are out of frame, although named: Jeff's father, and Hanif's mother. There's the absence of God too, who, even if he were in the poem, would not know the sound of abandonment the way a highway does.

While this poem is filled with people, there's a singular narrative voice that's clear and sure: a voice excited by musical associations, and in control of disclosure. In the voice of the speaker of the poem we are given detail: the model and colour of the car; the needle on that record player; the cigarette dancing on the lips; the hand trembling on the car wheel; the name of the highway; the wedding ring on a finger of that hand; the ring sacrificed on the road. All of this detail functions like sleight of hand, a trick, because right at the end, the poet's own grief slips in: 'and so maybe this is why my father would stare at the empty spaces my mother once occupied'. This ending is not just a poetic flourish; it's the main point. If Jeff's mother needed that song all those months after everything that happened, then maybe Hanif can find a music that'll work for his own grief too.

I feel so much respect and sadness for Jeff's mother. In the midst of everything she's carrying, here she is, driving her son and his friends around with the music on. Such is the love of mothers. When she pulls over in order to cry, it's hard not to cry with her. I think of what stories she might have told to her friends that night: *I was driving Jeff and his friends around and started crying and laughing uncontrollably when That Damned Song came on the radio.* Jeff's mother is everywhere: in the lives of those of us surviving what we thought we'd not find survivable. Meeting her in this poem, I wonder how many of my friends' parents were going through hell while my friends and I complained about how slow they drove. I'm now the age my friends' parents were when we were teenagers, and I wonder what my friends' parents saw in us in turn.

This poem's skill is shown in how casual the subject changes are – it's like a music documentary based on a personal story that, just when you think it's over, shows the viewer what the documentary has really been about all along. Stanzas interrupt themselves, little tributaries of stories spring out: Jeff seeking different warmth from two different women in one night is followed quickly by a reflection on what it means to become a man; and then we're back in the car, hearing about Neal Schon's guitar, and then we're back at a window with a man climbing out. What is abandonment? Who has been abandoned in the poem? So many people. And what's the music for that? Listen, Hanif Abdurraqib says, listen. It might help. And if it helps, that's enough.

The characters in this poem are moved by needs, some of them by a deep need for comfort, and the poem is an attempt to honour some sources of comfort. Nothing knows the sound of abandonment, and no warmth is warmth enough when you're left behind. Even the ghosts need help, most clearly the ghost that comes in at the end. What does that ghost need? To be coaxed out of the body; to be met with comfort, company and music.

I have bad asthma. So, at the start of the pandemic, when so little was known about whether asthmatics were at a greater risk or not, I began breathing exercises in earnest. It helped, a little. So did poetry: I always find that reading a book of poetry slows me down.

During Covid, many of us have thought a lot more about breathing than we did before. And many of us thought a lot more about hospital workers – porters, receptionists, cleaners, managers, administrators, doctors, fundraisers, nurses, ambulance drivers, paramedics – than we did before. What helps them? What keeps them breathing?

Leaving Early

Leanne O'Sullivan

My Love,
                    tonight Fionnuala is your nurse.
You'll hear her voice sing-song around the ward
lifting a wing at the shore of your darkness.
I heard that, in another life, she too journeyed
through a storm, a kind of curse, with the ocean
rising darkly around her, fierce with cold,
and no resting place, only the frozen
rocks that tore her feet, the light on her shoulders.

And no cure there but to wait it out.
If, while I'm gone, your fever comes down –
if the small, salt-laden shapes of her song
appear to you as a first glimmer of earth-light,
follow the sweet, hopeful voice of that landing.
She will keep you safe beneath her wing.

At the beginning of the pandemic, I began searching for poems about healthcare and came across this short one from Irish poet Leanne O'Sullivan. It's a poem written to her husband while he was in a coma, in the form of a letter one night when she's 'Leaving Early'.

There are so many reasons why a person would need to leave early – exhaustion; other duties; work; a shower; a rest; some air; some time to talk to someone; parenting; to meet a friend – but the poem carries anxiety, or even guilt. What if 'while I'm gone' something happens? Some small recovery, some small decline. Maybe the fever reduces, or spikes; maybe he'll emerge from the coma, only to go deeper down. The speaker of these lines has no way of knowing what might happen when she's away, and in the absence of knowing, she leaves her love in the care of the beloved nurse. 'She will keep you safe beneath her wing.'

In the spring of 2020, a friend who works in a hospital needed to use floor cleaner instead of hand sanitiser because all the sanitiser had been stolen. I heard of a ward manager in that same hospital who told her team that she loved them every day. Hospitals bring out all kinds of human behaviour: anxiety, yes, but also love.

This poem is from a book titled *A Quarter of an Hour*, which opens with a few paragraphs explaining that the poet's husband, following a brain infection, lost most of his memory and couldn't even recognise his wife: '[m]ore present and visual to him were the birds and wild animals that he believed he could see during his recovery.' Knowing that detail, this poem – beautiful without any of that background – takes on even more depth. The poet is speaking to her husband in the language of his dreams, directing his attention to the nurse, saying she's like a bird, 'lifting a wing at the shore of your darkness.'

The Irish myth the Children of Lír is about four siblings, the oldest of whom is named Fionnuala, meaning 'fair-shouldered' – implying someone with fair hair. In the myth, these four siblings were turned into swans – by a wicked stepmother, who else? – and damned to live in the cold lakes of Ireland forever. Fionnuala, the oldest sibling, prevented the curse from being permanent, making it so that the curse was only nine hundred years long. She also ensured that the siblings could retain their own voices. She weathered storms and freezing weather for nine centuries in the shape of a swan with huge wings; and here she is again, not in a myth, but in a poem, not in a lake, but in a ward. Fionnuala is, in one light, an older sister protecting her siblings from the worst of a curse, in another a trusted nurse helping a man through a coma. 'And no cure there but to wait it out.'

To write a poem that explores a myth so beautifully is one thing, but to write it in such a way that it doesn't exclude those unfamiliar with the myth is quite another. Whether a person knows the story of the Children of Lír or not, the poem's theme is one of love: for the patient, for the nurse, for the husband, for the self. Who was she, this nurse in hospital where the man was in such a terrible state of ill health? I think of the skill and care of that nurse and imagine that she, 'in another life', had her own troubles, her own woes, just like healthcare workers the world over during the pandemic: caring for people in their charge, and, at the same time, carrying their own concerns – families back home; friends back home; their own state of being. There is an economy of care in the poem: the kind of care that keeps you up at night. Alongside that, there's generosity, gratitude and hope; and all that awful waiting.

In a poem that carries such worry about the future, Leanne O'Sullivan turns to a myth for comfort. That's one of the functions of myth, not to tell the future, but to give meaning to the present. The oldest of four was able to help her siblings survive a curse; perhaps her namesake can do the same. Storms and strange animal shapes were not the final word in the story of lost loved ones; perhaps a husband can come back from strange places, too. Life became possible in an old story of unexplainable pain; perhaps life will be possible now as well.

Sometimes, younger LGBTQI+ friends of mine have asked if I'd teach them how to argue for their rights against conservative religious voices. I used to say no, because I want to work for a world where they don't have to argue for such rights. The burden shouldn't be on them.

I still have that hope. But these days I say yes.

Seventh Circle of Earth

Ocean Vuong

On 27 April 2011, a gay couple, Michael Humphrey and Clayton Capshaw, was murdered by immolation in their home in Dallas, Texas.

– DallasVoice

1

2

3

---

1. As if my finger, / tracing your collarbone / behind closed doors, / was enough / to erase myself. To forget / we built this house knowing / it won't last. How / does anyone stop / regret / without cutting / off his hands? / Another torch

2. streams through / the kitchen window, / another errant dove. / It's funny. I always knew / I'd be warmest beside / my man. / But don't laugh. Understand me / when I say I burn best / when crowned / with your scent: that earth-sweat / & Old Spice I seek out each night / the days

3. refuse me. / Our faces blackening / in the photographs along the wall. / Don't laugh. Just tell me the story / again, / of the sparrows who flew from falling Rome, / their blazed wings. / How ruin nested inside each thimbled throat / & made it sing

4

5

6

7

---

4. until the notes threaded to this / smoke rising / from your nostrils.
   Speak – / until your voice is nothing / but the crackle / of charred
5. bones. But don't laugh / when these walls collapse / & only
   sparks / not sparrows / fly out. / When they come / to sift through
   these cinders – & pluck my tongue, / this fisted rose, / charcoaled
   & choked / from your gone
6. mouth. / Each black petal / blasted / with what's left / of our
   laughter. / Laughter ashed / to air / to honey to baby / darling, /
   look. Look how happy we are / to be no one / & still
7. American.

The first thing you see in this poem is its presentation: the entire body of the poem pushed down to footnotes, written in small letters. Ocean Vuong's unusual choice of form embodies the poem's message: the blank architecture of the page speaks about what's missing, what's been placed below, what is kept under the surface.

'Seventh Circle of Earth' is a title that plays with the epic fourteenth-century poem *Inferno* by Dante. The *Inferno* details how the poet was guided through nine circles of hell, observing which sins are punished at each level. The seventh circle of hell is where sodomites, among others, suffer eternal torture. The epigraph at the beginning of the poem referencing the murder of an interracial gay couple – Michael Humphries and Clayton Capshaw – demonstrates how torture is not just the stuff of literature. It becomes clear why the title of the poem is 'Seventh Circle of Earth' not 'Seventh Circle of Hell'. Who needs the poetry of hell when queer folk are immolated in Texas?

There is a critical distance between what a society says safety looks like and what the actual experience of safety – or the lack of it – really is. And this poem, too, visualises the distance between things as they're said and things as they are: all that space on the page; all that pain and love forced underground.

Michael Humphrey and Clayton Capshaw didn't live out of view, but safety was out of their sights. It didn't exist. For them, hell was here. Their lives are a footnote, forgotten by many, but the poem amplifies their story, and exposes the fires they were subjected to. As subjects in Ocean Vuong's poem, they are not just victims, they are lovers. Lines like 'I always knew / I'd be warmest beside / my man' and 'your scent: that earth-sweat / & Old Spice I seek out each night' display the truth that their shared life was one of agency, desire and love; they were not just victims of horror. It's their voices we hear speaking, and they are all too aware of the world they live in. 'we built this house knowing / it won't last', one of them says: a terrible reminder of how formal policies about inclusion take a lifetime, or lifetimes, to sink into the marrow of a community.

In the face of violence the erotic is praised: 'When they come / to sift through these cinders – & pluck my tongue, / this fisted rose, / charcoaled & choked / from your gone // mouth.' Fire is not the only thing that burned this couple: their love burned too. Their laughter hangs in the air like a memory, like an accusation. They are consumed in love for each other, and they are consumed by fire because of their love.

This is an underworld poem, and as such is in conversation with many mythologies and poems set in the underworld. In mythology and poetry, the underworld always reveals the overworld: it's an exposé of the real. The underworld knows that people are murdered because wider populations cannot stand the idea of queer love. The form of 'Seventh Circle of Earth' shows how everything below the line is true above the line too: the love of the couple, and their death by immolation.

The final word – 'American' – is breathtaking. It is a demanding poem, a confronting poem: a lullaby sung by a couple while they're burning for their love. 'Laughter ashed

/ to air / to honey to baby / darling'. The poem could have ended there. But it continues, forcing our attention not towards any hell, but towards earth:

> Look how happy we are / to be no one / & still
> 7. American.

They are 'no one' – discardable, thrown away, under the surface; they are also 'still' – unmoving; and they are 'American'. This juxtaposition of being invisible yet visible; of being initiated into a ritual of belonging, even if that ritual of belonging is violent; of pride in a country even if that country takes no pride in you. This is what Ocean Vuong highlights as an American nightmare. He doesn't end this poem by making this a story about a one-time event in a one-time place; he ends this poem by making it a poem about a dream: a real one, the American one. What will people have to live through – or die through – in order to belong? In these final lines, this poem is an indictment in the form of a lullaby, sung by men facing their own end.

Poetry has taught me that it can choose the most unexpected places to pause. Sometimes, rather than going for the extraordinary moment of drama, or eros, or shock, a poem will show the small moment – simply to examine what's happening, to look a few layers deep. Such poems are written around a pause. They let an ordinary moment show everything it holds.

Song

Tracy K. Smith

I think of your hands all those years ago
Learning to maneuvre a pencil, or struggling
To fasten a coat. The hands you'd sit on in class,
The nails you chewed absently. The clumsy authority
With which they'd sail to the air when they knew
You knew the answer. I think of them lying empty
At night, of the fingers wrangling something
From your nose, or buried in the cave of your ear.
All the things they did cautiously, pointedly,
Obedient to the suddenest whim. Their shames.
How they failed. What they won't forget year after year.
Or now. Resting on the wheel or the edge of your knee.
I am trying to decide what they feel when they wake up
And discover my body is near. Before touch.
Pushing off the ledge of the easy quiet dancing between us.

This love poem by Tracy K. Smith is written about – and even to – the hands of a lover. The poem starts in the unknown childhood of this person: 'I think of your hands all those years ago'. These hands have been busy since childhood: 'Learning to maneuver a pencil, or struggling / To fasten a coat.' These hands have been raised or kept hidden in class. The poem is seeking to remember the past that was not known to the poet: the past of acquiring skills, the things kept hidden by those hands, the things revealed.

We can think of the hands at all stages of growth: the hands of a child, the hands of an adult, being the same yet somehow different. The hands are ageing, the hands are learning, the hands are doing things in private, the hands are controlled and spontaneous, the hands have been hands every day of this person's life. To explore a person's life through their hands is an intimate thing: unknown worlds are opened up through this attention.

When I fell in love with Paul, I was overwhelmed with attention towards unexpected things. One morning I looked at the cups we'd drunk tea from the night before. They were on a coffee table. I remember staring at them, thinking that I wanted to look at everything they meant. The cup he'd touched, had drunk from. I remember feeling foolish. Then I remember not caring. The point was love, and even a piece of pottery could hold it. I took a photo of the cups – I have it still.

Tracy K. Smith could have written about the lover's ears, or eyes, or lips. She could just have written about the lover's personality. Instead she trains her eyes – and ours – on the hands as a portal to the person: their lessons, their learning, their habits, their privacies, spontaneities, shames, achievements and failures. She is talking about so much more than the hands. Poetry, for a very long time, used fancy words to describe something when a plain word would do. *Periphrasis* this practice is called; using many words in place of a single one. For a long time, it was a feature of poetry, but it's less popular now – there's a preference for plainer language. This poem doesn't use ornamental language to describe hands, instead preferring a direct approach. Such simple language is not reductive, however: sometimes to show a thing with clarity helps its many possible meanings to shine.

In 'Song' there's a deliberate ambiguity, where more than one thing is being said at once. *Who are you?* this poem asks over and over; *Who were you when you were younger? Who are you when you're alone? Who are you when we're together? Who are you when we wake; when you reach for me in bed?* But these questions aren't directly answered: the poem contains privacy and intimacy, stretching out and holding back.

A friend of mine had a baby, and just after she'd given birth, her child was put on her bare chest. *Hallo Stranger,* my friend said to her as-yet-unnamed daughter. Later she told me that for a short instant, she was shocked that the first thing she'd called her daughter was *Stranger.* But then the shock passed; her daughter was a stranger, loved and unknown. All love has strangeness and space in it. All connections have distance. We cannot possess each other, even when we try. We touch each other, or lie in each other's arms, or we shake each other's hand, or hug, or wave, or tear a sandwich in half for sharing, or wipe a tear away, or scratch each other's back. All of these are activities of the hands, Tracy K. Smith reminds us in 'Song', and there are unexplored stories in the story of a person and their hands: their hands for themselves; their hands with one other.

The poem is titled 'Song'. It could have been named 'Hands', or 'Your Hands', or 'Before Touch', or any one of many other titles. Why 'Song'? Is their shared love like a song? Is the space between them a song? As the poem ends, the location has moved to the intimacy of a bed. The speaker wonders what the hands are feeling when they wake – it's the *hands* that wake, not the lover – and reach for her body. 'Pushing off the ledge of the easy quiet dancing between us.' That verb *dancing* echoes the 'Song' of the title. There is music between the poet and the owner of these hands.

Perhaps a poem about a lover's hands could easily centre on anxiety about previous partners, but there isn't such anxiety here. Instead there's a generous curiosity about everything that's unknown. In such an intimate poem, there is a tension between disclosure and quiet. 'Song' does not describe the kind of relationship between the lovers, nor does it concern itself with a physical description of the lover's hands: are their fingers long or short? Are the hands strong or elegant? Are they hairy or smooth? Does the lover still bite their nails? The voice of the poem is one of love. Instead of description, we're given wonder. Instead of seeing the storyline of the couple laid out, we see the lover's hands, that most tender instrument of body language. We hear the music of touch between them. A song is implied but not sung: a public poem about a private life.

I've written so many angry poems over the years. They help me a lot, by channelling all that energy into something creative. However, I rarely show them to anyone. After a few days – or weeks, or months – I return to them and realise how limited they were. So I have deep admiration for angry poems that make it to publication. An angry poem that's gone from needing to be written to needing to be shared is a thing of power and magnificence.

Coconut Oil

Roshni Goyate

Vatika bottle sits in the bathroom,
contents solidified by London's night.
Mum microwaves it to a clear sap –
an ancestral ritual improvised.

She sits me down, braids unplaited,
drags plastic comb through my hair.
Ouch Mummy, Mummy not too hard!
Pretends my squeaks are not there.

Drip-drip onto my invisible scalp.
Grap-grip with the palms of her hand.
Rub-rub rub-rub taming flyaways.
Slap-slip onto the slick-dark of strands.

A soft scent, sweet and buttery, slippery
tinged with metallic sweat of my brow,
provokes questions in the playground,
Why do you smell so funny? How?

The powder-red shame of coconut oil
spray-paints itself onto my skin.
I delete it from life like a bad line of code,
no chance of it coming back in.

When suddenly, this hair oil that gave me such grief
comes back for wellbeing's bright new age.
No longer smelling funny, a great white commodity
marked up for organic food shops. All the rage.

This poem by Roshni Goyate sets itself up with the kind of musical chime you can well imagine a classroom of children reciting:

She **sits** me **down**, || **braids** un**plait**ed,
drags **pla**stic **comb** || **through** my **hair**.
Ouch Mummy, **Mummy** || **not** too **hard**!
Pre**tends** my **squeaks** || are not **there**.

The beats in this poem – called *iambs* – lend themselves to easy recitation. Later on, in the next stanza, the poem contains *onomatopoeia*, where the word sounds like the thing it's describing: drip-drip; grap-grip, rub-rub, slap-slip. It can be fashionable to disparage poems that make use of such sonic and percussive techniques, but I love what contemporary poets are doing by reclaiming such practices, often associated with poetry for children, to convey fury, or other adult ambivalences, within a poem. In this way, Roshni Goyate is alongside poets like Patience Agbabi and Don Paterson, whose work often follows very strict form, with surprising results. Picture a classroom of children reciting a poem they've learnt off by heart. Before hearing the words, you can hear the singsong quality of their voices. Now go nearer, and you realise their innocent voices are reciting a poem about climate change, or reparations, or feminism.

The poem turns: there's mocking in the playground. 'Why do you smell so funny? How?' another pupil demands. There is such raw power in the *How?* It's from a voice that says *answer to me*; a voice that assumes attention and belonging, self-appointed and confident of its authority to be so. Children can say terrible things, but there's an old drama repeated here: a child learns lessons in the playground about culture, dominance, fitting in and erasure; a child repeats what they've heard at home.

The speaking voice of the poet ages and matures as the poem progresses: shame arrives – the recognition of visibility 'spray-paints itself onto my skin'; then the adult register of a computer programmer: 'I delete it from life like a bad line of code'; and the sound of a poet promising herself never to put herself in a situation of such shame again. The voice that cried 'Mummy, Mummy' is gone. The speaker has matured – from innocence to confusion to shame to resolution – and learns to delete. What's deleted? Initially: connection with parents, with family tradition, with ancestors; a sense of citizenship; an expectation of safety. That Goyate communicates all of this while maintaining the plinky-plonk percussion of a childlike poem is a brilliant feat of irony. Form often serves function, and in 'Coconut Oil' the function of the form is to speak about the terrible things children learn, and the terrible things children say. Someone has asserted themselves as the authority on How to Behave, How to Act, How to Pass, How to Be One of Us. Are we talking about an empire or a classroom? Yes.

The final stanza in this poem is – even visually – different. The lines are longer, and it can be easy to stumble when trying to maintain the same chime as the previous stanzas. The poem has stepped out of the time zone of a child, too, even the time zone of a single speaker. The world is now the stage of this poem, and the actors are no longer children but enact whiteness, capitalism, manipulative marketing. The coconut oil that had been the justification for exclusion in Roshni Goyate's childhood is shown for sale, at a marked-up price, in organic food shops and wellbeing centres. *They were right! Amazing! It's good for white people too!* is the message informing these lines. The goalposts have shifted, and what was considered worthy of exclusion is now just considered worthy. No wonder the poem finishes off with those three extraordinary words: 'All the rage.'

'All the rage' can have a few meanings. A new style of footwear can be all the rage one summer, and in this poem, yes, suddenly coconut oil is all the rage. But the poem goes beneath the passing trends of marketing into anger. Who gets to decide what's acceptable for some families to do? Roshni Goyate's poem evolves from a classroom chant to a cultural exposé. It is, in a certain sense, an adult voice speaking back to their childhood self, saying that *yes,* what was experienced in the playground was not only the usual taunts of school years, but the embodied voice of whiteness telling you that you'll only fit in if you pass the arbitrary standards for inclusion: now you're one of us, now you're not; now you're foreign, now you're fashionable.

The poem isn't just about what happens amongst kids – as if such things are only mild. It's saying that what happens amongst kids is what happens in the workplace, in society, in the voice of a government, in the voices of economics, marketing and citizenship. The voice that speaks out in this poem is one that can code and decode; it's a voice that looks at the codification of diversity and wonders about the economics and presumption behind such marketing trends. It's a voice that asks 'at what cost?', with all the meanings that holds. It's a voice that rises, in its own power, asking questions of authority, and sitting with its own rage.

When I was eleven, I met my first Protestant. Her name was Bernie. She was kind and warm and good. She was a leader at some youth events I'd been going to. *She's a Protestant*, my mother said to me, *they're wrong.* And a new world was born in me. I felt sorry for Bernie, and imagined her on fire. I remember hating that this was true. I feared for her. I pitied her for belonging to the wrong.

The Place Where We Are Right

Yehuda Amichai
(Trans. Stephen Mitchell)

From the place where we are right
flowers will never grow
in the spring.

The place where we are right
is hard and trampled
like a yard.

But doubts and loves
dig up the world
like a mole, a plow.
And a whisper will be heard in the place
where the ruined
house once stood.

Yehuda Amichai is probably the most famous Israeli poet of the twentieth century. He lived from 1924 to 2000 and was celebrated both in Israel and around the world. Often his work is characterised by a style of language that's distilled from complexity to simplicity. He was published and translated widely, and even in translation, his work is filled with elegance and poise and power and music and insight. I only studied Biblical Hebrew for one semester at university. Reading Yehuda Amichai makes me wish I could understand these poems in their original sound.

'The Place Where We Are Right', translated by Stephen Mitchell, is one of Amichai's most known and loved poems. It sets up a simple rhythm: the repetition of the title – six single-syllable words – repeated three times before you're halfway through: the place where we are right, the place where we are right, the place where we are right.

Where is the emphasis of this line? Is it the *place* where we are right? Or the place where *we* are right? Or the place where we are *right*? Depending as to how you place the stress, the interest of this poem could be location or group belonging or ideology. This simple phrase is malleable, and that's what I think is meant.

When I was sixteen, I was at a church summer festival. Thousands of earnest young people camping in a field. Evenings at the festival often featured a debate about what was deemed a controversial topic: Can Christians listen to secular music? Are my Catholic neighbours going to hell? Are Freemasons really Christian? You can see both trend and premise: Christianity and its borders. The debates considered how certain things – music, Masons and Catholics – were all dodgy until proven tolerable. I'd gone from pitying Protestants to loving them, and I was desperate to fit in. That particular summer, I was at the festival debate about Freemasons. There were four men on the stage (men: another theme). Two Freemasons argued that Christianity and Freemasonry were compatible; two other men asserted that Christianity and Freemasonry were incompatible. I had never heard of Freemasons. I had no idea what was going on. I had a vague recollection that masonry had something to do with stones. I turned to one of my new friends. *Whose side are we on?* I asked him. He hesitated. Then pointed to the men arguing against the Freemasons. *Theirs*, he said, and my mind was made up. There were about two thousand young people at this debate. I booed and hissed at the Freemasons with the rest of the crowd; I felt anger when the Freemasons made a reasonable point – how dare they speak in a compelling way? – and I cheered at the end to indicate which team had 'won', as if there was ever a doubt, given the make-up of the audience. After the debate, when the Freemasons were driving away, many of us surrounded their car, faking fond farewells, slapping the car, pushing it a little, jeering. Later on, back at the campfire with my friends, we spoke about who'd made the best points. I remember saying our side had been quite gracious. The gorgeous power of that word: *our.*

After I trained as a conflict mediator, I specialised working with groups, and often, in the context of this work, I'd refer-ence my own carnal sectarianism by telling this story about the festival and the Masons, the booing and the powerful belonging. Once, I referenced this incident and I noticed a man in the room – it was a small group; only ten people – go pale. 'I was one of those two Freemasons,' he said, and everything stopped. 'I've never been as frightened in my life.' Then he spoke about being jeered at by crowds of young people, feeling the hostility of the devout surge against him. He said he didn't stop shaking for hours after the experience, and that it took him years – in fact, decades – to feel safe enough to talk about it.

From the place where we are right
flowers will never grow

Yehuda Amichai's poem speaks to me about the allure of that *place*, that place where rightness confirms belonging, and where, with that confirmation, anything else is possible. The promise of this place is that it'll be fruitful, it'll be safe, it'll yield community and belonging and intelligence and right reason; but this promise will not last: flowers will fail, even in the spring.

In many ways, what Amichai does in this poem is bring a concrete imagination to the places of ideological bonding. It's almost as if he's responding to a prompt: *Describe your political opinions using only agricultural metaphors . . .* and he does it, but then goes further: he critiques the landscape; notes what's needed to make it flourish; hints at the erasures embedded on this landscape; hears a whisper.

In conflict negotiation – especially when politically or religiously infused– there are many layers, and those layers need all kinds of attention. In the conflict resolution world, there are many approaches: human encounter, political nego-tiation, policy development, historical enquiry, education projects, art projects and so on. Amichai makes his own suggestion about how the hard and flowerless fields of resist-ance can be made bountiful, offering 'doubts and loves'. To doubt the story you have inherited; to love someone from another side. It's not the only conflict-resolution technique, but some version of this can be akin to a conversion of the heart that has motivated many to begin processes of acknowl-edgement, reparation, policy and political change. Love is not the daisy-chain answer in this poem. Love and doubt are the motivations for the work that's necessary for change. The world needs to be dug up, he says, and then points to a mole, or a machine.

Yehuda Amichai has embedded, or buried, a deep respect for the past – particularly the eradicated past – in this poem. In excavating it – like a farmer, like a mole – we might encounter something else, something that our imagination of rightness had denied. There were *ruins* here once, he suggests, 'where the ruined / house once stood.' Somebody in the past saw a ruin and thought that it would tell a story, so they destroyed the ruin: tried to hide the past. Amichai isn't only talking about the house that once stood, or even the ruins that once stood; but the whispers that remain of those ruins. What whispers are they, he wonders, as this poem ends. It's easy to think he's being naive, but he's not, he's being brave; saying that such human experiences are at the very core of examining dangerous fundamentalisms. In his vision, doubt and love – what glorious partners they are – can energise the powerful work of hearing what has been hitherto denied.

Why doubts *and* loves? Why wouldn't love be enough?

Because it never has been. Love has been the motivation for many terrible things: people have killed and denied and excluded and hated in the name of love. To write a poem like this is to take a risk: Yehuda Amichai may have faced accusations of being traitorous, of minimising grief, or difference. Poetry, in this sense, is a lonely art, written by a person with a sense that more must be done. 'The Place Where We Are Right' is political in the sense that it is profoundly personal, and in that personal drive, he is asking questions of citizenship. Lonely indeed. Brave too. People – like me, in a tent with thousands of other young people – feel a deep sense of belonging, a deep sense of love, by deciding on a mutual enemy. I didn't need more love, or even better love. I needed *doubt*: of myself, of my belonging, of my friends, of the story I was telling.

I was a lonely child, given to reading and daydreaming. I would read about people and dream about meeting them. I would watch people and dream about being their friend. It's not a bad school for poetry, but it did make for some solitary years.

I understand the drama – and crisis – of imagining my own loneliness as unique. It was, it wasn't. It is true, it isn't all true. Everyone is alone, and everyone is alone in their own way. In this, we are together.

What You Missed that Day You Were Absent from Fourth Grade

Brad Aaron Modlin

Mrs Nelson explained how to stand still and listen
to the wind, how to find meaning in pumping gas,

how peeling potatoes can be a form of prayer. She took
questions on how not to feel lost in the dark.

After lunch she distributed worksheets
that covered ways to remember your grandfather's

voice. Then the class discussed falling asleep
without feeling you had forgotten to do something else –

something important – and how to believe
the house you wake in is your home. This prompted

Mrs Nelson to draw a chalkboard diagram detailing
how to chant the Psalms during cigarette breaks,

and how not to squirm for sound when your own thoughts
are all you hear; also, that you have enough.

The English lesson was that *I am*
is a complete sentence.

And just before the afternoon bell, she made the math equation
look easy. The one that proves that hundreds of questions,

and feeling cold, and all those nights spent looking
for whatever it was you lost, and one person

add up to something.

The title of Brad Aaron Modlin's poem, 'What You Missed that Day You Were Absent from Fourth Grade', has a mild melodrama to it. Anyone who is a teacher knows you have to repeat, repeat, repeat, because there's always a child absent. And even the ones who were present were probably only half paying attention. So, whatever you say, say it three times a day, for a few weeks. However, this poem imagines a world where one day, a teacher teaches all the necessary things for a life: how to find meaning, how to pray, how to live after grief, how to be at ease with yourself, how to be yourself. One pupil was away from school that day, and now, years later, in the voice of an adult, comes this explanation of all the things they missed on that day of absence.

Who hasn't felt left out? This poem is for all of us.

Reading this poem, I find myself thinking of the ways in which I've felt like a failure as an adult, and imagining that those failures were because I missed the day that lesson was taught at school: when was the day we were taught that gay boys are boys too? When was the day we were taught that loving poetry was enough? When was the day we learnt that feeling desperately lonely, even when you're ten, is okay? What's the lesson for letting you know that looking at everyone else's family and judging your own – feeling like they're all together and you're all apart – is okay?

If you were to ask someone, 'In your life, what are five ways you've felt like you didn't get the lesson or memo everybody else got?' you'd end up having a very interesting conversation. We all feel left out in different ways, it seems. *Nobody told me to expect this,* we'd hear. *I never knew I'd feel so out of my depth,* someone would say. *When will this feel normal?* someone will ask, and someone else will say, *How do I survive the not-knowing?* Welcome to the world.

Into this reality about the truth of being an adult, Brad Aaron Modlin introduces Mrs Nelson, a teacher who, even though these things can't be taught, nevertheless taught all of these things. If there were such a class, and such a teacher, what disaster it would be to miss this day of lessons. It is both a consolation to know the learning could happen, and a devastation to know you missed out on it. Of course, there is no Mrs Nelson. The brilliance of the poem is that by imagining that there could be such a person, we have a stand-in for a perfect teacher, some wise angel with chalk and schoolbooks to teach us all the things we need in order to fit into our own lives.

In this world, Mrs Nelson taught her class 'how to chant the Psalms during cigarette breaks'. Someone objected to this poem on social media once; their comment was something like: *What kind of corrupt teacher would teach kids to smoke? Someone needs to report that teacher to the authorities.* They had thought the poem was literal. And, while I initially laughed, and then wanted to correct them, I stopped and took them seriously for a moment. I liked their misunderstanding – a misunderstanding that took a whimsical poem and made it even more outrageous. Someone taught everyone how to be cool, how to adult, how to cope with grief. In this supposed reading, some teacher thought: *To hell with the curriculum, I'm going to teach you all how to be alive. Take out your lighters, everyone.* Sure, it may be a misreading of the poem, but even misreadings of a poem should be taken seriously. And also: report that teacher, give them a sentence; give them a medal.

Mrs Nelson is, no doubt, a fantasy, but there's truth in the poem, because Brad has validated everyone who feels like they missed those lessons. Lurking in the blank space of this poem is a kindness, a response to the fear of missing out that is felt the world over: it's okay, me too.

When I was eleven, I met a youth worker. He was from Belfast; I'm from Cork. Aldo Magliocco was this youth work-er's name. Aldo became a real friend to me. I was eleven, he was – well, I don't know – thirty, or sixty; it was all the same. He would phone up my parents and say, 'I'm driving to different youth camps around the country for the next two weeks; will I take Pádraig?' I loved it. I got to drive around Ireland sitting in the passenger seat of his amazing Saab, and he would let me roll the windows up and down. We'd talk about books, and he'd tell me about pranks his friends played on him at university. He was a nice man, the kind of youth worker any person would want in the life of a lonely child. He asked real questions and he listened. 'What do you think about religion?' he asked me. Because I wanted to impress him I'd only brought holy books to read. 'Do you read other kinds of books?' he asked me. I wondered what the right answer was. He wasn't teaching me to be an adult; he was giving me permission to be a child. In a department store once, he was buying a t-shirt and he asked me my size so he could buy one for me too. I couldn't bear the goodness. I said my mother wouldn't allow it.

I stayed in touch with him over the years. He moved back to Italy, where his family were from. He'd bring English language students to Cork for language intensives, and I'd call round and hang out with them. A few years ago, I was in New York City, and I got a text from another old friend to say, 'Aldo's just died.' It was a freezing night, lots of rain. I suppose the rain was good, because it washed all my tears away. I looked back at my own self through the lens of this man who had just died, and found myself filled with the gratitude that Aldo Magliocco was a person who brought me into my own life. I didn't have a Mrs Nelson, but I did have an Aldo.

This could have been a comfortless poem, but somehow it's the opposite. It's the genius of Brad Aaron Modlin to create a poem about feeling left out that somehow makes you feel seen. He felt alone in moments throughout his life, and whilst his isolations aren't my isolations, somehow this poem turns – with great respect – to isolations everywhere.

Love poetry doesn't try to describe the entirety of the love between the writer and their beloved, nor does it work as a manual for intimacy. Love poetry often opens up a story of love by looking at a single moment between lovers: a time of intimacy, or frustration; a description of the nape of their neck; the feel of their hand on your back; the space they leave in the bed when they're away; the presence – or absence – of each other's anxieties.

Life Drawing

R. A. Villanueva

How she is quiet before his robe falls
each week to his ankles. This man who sits, nude
for my wife, whom she draws with Conté sticks

and pastel pencils. Each page in her notebook
is a parade of his torsos, galley proofs
of breastbones and chests. She explains

because these lines are my favorite
and shows me, traces with her knuckle tip
chin to sternum, jaw to shoulder, clavicle to cusp

of the arm. How in three passes
an artist makes a place for a head
to rest. Later, in blue and orange

pigments mixed at the edge of a knife, thinned
with linseed oil and mineral spirits,
my wife will paint him on a canvas

primed black. Again his body will end
just above the pelvis, will fade
into a fog of armrest or shadow, cushion

or hip as if rendered in some fugitive dye.
Because he is only the second man I have seen naked,
in person. His, just the third I have seen in my life.

When I tell my wife I want to write about her
naked, sketch her back's faint taper
as a class might to check perspective, describe

the moles I notice on the underside of a breast
as we make love, she says I can. And, in return,
she will paint the whole of me, bare

from the neck down as I pose
in our living room. *No one will even know
this is you. The light will blank out your face.*

This poem by R. A. Villanueva is filled with intimacy and anxiety, skill and observation. It's a poem about a certain kind of masculinity, as well as a poem about marriage, vulnerability and trust.

The poem is in three parts, and each focuses on a different body. The first turn is the longest one: we hear of the poet's wife as she observes and then sketches the nude body of a male model. In the second turn the poet wants to write a poem about his wife's naked body. And then finally, just at the end, the woman in the poem turns the gaze back on the poet and asks him to pose naked for her. A parade of bodies, each gazed at with respect, but two of the bodies – that of the woman and the model – seem comfortable in the gaze, whereas the speaker's voice is one of comparison, vulnerability and self-consciousness. The voice of the poem is filled, perhaps, with a fear of disappearing if looked at directly.

What can we say we know about the woman in the poem? She's skilled, and is comfortable talking about bodies and intimacies and limitations. She keeps count: '*he is only the second man I have seen naked, / in person. His, just the third I have seen in my life.*' The modesty of the numbers – two and three – are narrated with ease. Her gaze is not predatory. She has favourite bodylines – she traces them with the tip of her knuckle: '*chin to sternum, jaw to shoulder, clavicle to cusp // of the arm.*' Hers is a gaze of appreciation not appropriation, a distinguishing gaze, not a diminishing one. She is sketching the model as she sees him, with no imagination of conquest. When her husband wishes to write about her naked – almost like he's painting with words – she consents, but continues her steady gaze, initiating reciprocity, as if to say: *let's look at each other through our art*. This reciprocity is an invitation to trust, but notably, not just trust between the spouses, but a trust of self. She, we have gathered already, is steady, but the speaker seems uncomfortable at the idea of standing naked in the room. She seeks to reassure him: '*No one will even know / this is you. The light will blank out your face.*' What we don't know is whether he takes this as a comfort or an erasure. Maybe he *wants* to be known – maybe that's the small worry at the heart of this poem.

The disrobing at the beginning of the poem is one marked by consent and art. It is intimate, because our bodies are intimate, but it is neither crude nor clinical. Somebody is being paid to be a model, and the artist is quiet 'before his robe falls / . . . to his ankles.' The encounter is for the purpose of learning how to sketch a body. But the poet's voice enters in, and the poet's voice is worried about how to categorise the intimacy. The poet is looking at the sketch, as well as imagining his wife looking at the model. The poet is taking this personally. The poser is doing something for the painter that excludes the poet. The naked man is sketched with pastel pencils, and the pages of her notebooks contain a parade of his torsos. (All the *p*'s: my god, how many ways can a poet avoid saying *penis*?)

The presence of the absence of a penis in a poem about its presence is a thing of comedy and vulnerability, with alliteration being a hint about the unspoken focus of anxiety in the poem. Even though his wife's sketches end just above the pelvis, the husband pays attention to what's down below.

Letting an echo of *p, p, p, p* be heard without that *p* being conjugated into the word, R. A. Villanueva shows an extraordinary artistry of constraint. Rather than voice anxiety head-on, he lets the voice of anxiety speak – in this case a percussion of *p* sounds – intimating the concerns the speaker is too worried to voice. You could call this a certain allusive alliteration, where the repeated *p*'s don't just build a pattern, but hint at something that is never fully shown in the poem. There are many things unsaid about the body, the poem tells us.

What is this anxiety? Comparison? Competition? Is the speaker jealous that the model's body is a shape that's more admirable or attractive? Or is he uncomfortable admiring the model's body? Or is the poem about being comfortable with your body – whatever its shape – and outside of the echo chamber of comparison? We don't know.

At the start of this poem the voice of the speaker seemed almost possessive, with a small echo of some old masculinist form of anxiety about 'my wife'. But the reciprocity of the poem changes that. In the poem, consent, sensuality, knowledge and beholding become mutual. Questions about comparison or competition fade away. There are no excuses made for having the body you have, only two people each using their art to gather what they see when they see each other. The poem offers an invitation to consider such intimacies, vulnerabilities and anxieties in our lives; to consider where and with whom our bodies are fluent; to let the story of the body be a story of love, between ourselves and our chosen others.

For many years I kept up a correspondence with a friend, Bryan. He'd moved to work in the far north of Canada, a place accessible only by plane. Every two weeks supplies would be flown in, together with post. 'Can you make sure there's a letter for me on those planes?' he asked.

Both of us loved poetry, and often the letters contained copies of poems we were working on.

I've kept all those letters. I could recognise Bryan's handwriting anywhere.

Consider the Hands that Write this Letter

Aracelis Girmay

after Marina Wilson

Consider the hands
that write this letter.
Left palm pressed flat against paper,
as we have done before, over my heart,
in peace or reverence to the sea,
some beautiful thing
I saw once, felt once: snow falling
like rice flung from the giants' wedding,
or strangest of strange birds. & consider, then,
the right hand, & how it is a fist,
within which a sharpened utensil,
similar to the way I've held a spade,
the horse's reins, loping, the very fists
I've seen from roads through Limay & Estelí.
For years, I have come to sit this way:
one hand open, one hand closed,
like a farmer who puts down seeds & gathers up;
food will come from that farming.
Or, yes, it is like the way I've danced
with my left hand opened around a shoulder,
my right hand closed inside
of another hand. & how I pray,
I pray for this to be my way: sweet
work alluded to in the body's position to its paper:
left hand, right hand
like an open eye, an eye closed:
one hand flat against the trapdoor,
the other hand knocking, knocking.

The setting for this elegant poem is a poet at a desk or table, writing. Her left hand is open, pressing on the table, her right hand 'is a fist, / within which a sharpened utensil'. A pencil. What is she writing? A letter, the title implies, but a letter to whom? Herself? Her future? Someone else? Could it also be a poem?

'Consider the Hands that Write this Letter' is a poetic self-portrait of the artist at work. The focus is the act of writing, and while much about the speaker's life is referenced – her love of the sea, snow, birds, horseriding, travel, dancing – these details are not the final point of the poem. Rather the poem is interested in the poet as they write: what's happening, what they're doing, what they're resisting, what they're holding together. Writing is physical, and the poem's focus is activity of hands during the act of writing: the push-and-pull of energy, the tension created and sustained for creative purposes.

When a person writes by hand, Aracelis Girmay suggests in this poem, they place one open hand on the table – just like a person might have a hand placed on the heart while watching a beautiful sunset – and their other hand is closed – like when 'I've held a spade / the horse's reins'. The open hand indicates receptivity, the closed hand has work to do. These two hands are not separate, of course, they are the body of the speaker. The poem joins these two hands together: looking at a person dancing, a person praying.

Openhandedness and closehandedness, 'an open eye, an eye closed', waiting and working . . . all of these things are contained in the body.

A poem about poetry is called an *ars poetica,* a term referencing a poem written by the Roman poet Quintus Horatius Flaccus (65-8 BCE) also known as Horace. His ars poetica – a letter-poem written in strict form – is an introduction to the art of poetry: writing it, reading it, learning how to describe the art of it. All his subsequent poems about poetry are gathered under the title of Horace's *Ars Poetica.* Sometimes such poems are about the *idea* of poetry, sometimes – as in Aracelis Girmay's poem – they're about the very act of writing poetry, what that requires from a person and their body.

I sometimes worry that writing about writing can run the risk of separating the world into those who do and those who don't. However, Aracelis Girmay doesn't fall into that trap. 'Consider the Hands that Write this Letter' sees poetry as just one of the modes involving open-hand/closed-hand postures. The speaker in this poem invites readers to notice resistance and desire in their bodies, and to notice the necessary tensions involved in going about even the most everyday of tasks: parenting, being in love, going to work, being alone.

The poem's ending is arresting: 'one hand flat against the trapdoor, / the other hand knocking, knocking.' What trapdoor? It's a courageous thing to add a new image into the final lines of a poem. The trapdoor is the page, and the speaker of the poem is both curious and cautious about what's beneath it. Why would you knock? In the hope that something will respond? What would that be? – a story? Another self? Something locked away? Some unresolved thread of self that needs to be expressed? Something that should be dead?

This is a poem of great elegance, even gentleness, with images of dancing and beauty. But it's also a poem of wildness: horses, strange birds, sharp blades to sharpen pencils. We hear that the project of writing unlocks things you might have put away, lets voices you may have wished to quieten be heard, gives language to that which might have been unconscious.

Of the game *Hide and Seek* the British child psychoanalyst D. W. Winnicott wrote, 'it is a joy to be hidden, and disaster not to be found.' I find myself thinking of this phrase whenever I think about Aracelis Girmay's trapdoor. Something is hiding, and is seeking to be found. There is a playfulness, a riskiness, a curiosity and danger in the process of seeking that which has been hidden. I love the image of a poet pushing with one hand, and pulling with the other.

Underneath this poem is the question *Why?* Why does a person feel the need to write? The speaker in this poem is opening and closing at the same time, is in the telling-yet-not-telling tension that's at the heart of communication. This isn't just about craft, or editing. The energy of this poem is one of knowledge: the knowledge of how much your writing can reveal of you, how much it can feel like a necessary risk.

For years my partner Paul and I have run a storytelling night in Belfast. We choose a theme and invite people to submit a true story from their own life on that theme. The event is not aimed at professionals, it's aimed at people who have something they wish to tell, something true. Once, a man who was due to tell a story asked to speak to me before the event. 'I'm not sure if people will accept me. Will they hate me?' I'd read his story, and knew the audience would love him. I reassured him as best I could. But I knew that his worry was something deeper than performance anxiety. He too had one hand opening, one hand closing: he'd been compelled to write something from his life, and he knew he was revealed in what he'd written. His resistance in turn revealed that he'd done the true work of writing. He was on both sides of the trapdoor. Aracelis Girmay is, too: knocking and holding, wondering what's inside, wondering how to contain it, or release it. Her words come from the outside and the inside. She's praying, and she's the answer to her prayers. She's the one knocking, she's the one opening.

Learning about the Renaissance as a teenager introduced me to the term *perspective*, particularly the ways that art of that era demonstrated the capacity to represent three-dimensional objects on the two-dimensional plane of a canvas.

Perspective isn't only for painting, though: perspective is part of the fact of being human. Looking into my own stories of the past, I can see more now than I could then. Time makes space: for honesty, or insight, or confession. I've learnt much from poets who look to their own past, naming now what they didn't – or couldn't – name then.

Living in the Past

Joy Ladin

San Francisco 1982–1992

The views were what everyone had:

hills, parades of paper dragons,
the prison surrounded by sugar water.
Tourists laughed in the crumbling showers.

Climate? Mild. No fear, no regret. Life
stared like a lizard, blinking back
the salt of our climaxes.

Outside, the epidemic spread.
Ten years.
We sipped champagne

from small black bottles, followed manicured paths
between trees that had lost their bark
and smelled like medicine. I wish

I'd kissed you then. You seemed distracted
as we crossed the shell
of the band that only played anthems.

It wasn't hot but you dripped
hard bright beads of sweat.
The newly infected slumped on benches,

a garden of vanishing plants.
You seemed to be staring at their shoes.
I'm seeing stars, you said.

During the coronavirus pandemic I was talking with a friend, a scientist. She – so fluent to the terminologies most of the rest of us were only just becoming familiar with – was curious about epidemiology. DNA coding is her area, but as the pandemic started, she began looking at the patterns of past pandemics in order to estimate how long this one would drag on. Three months? That seemed outrageous in April of 2020. Six months? A year? More?

My friend thought she'd turn to the influenza of the 1900s for information: the Spanish Flu of 1918–1919 caused 20–50 million deaths alone. She was shocked, however, to reckon with a more recent 'global epidemic' (as it's called): HIV. It wasn't that she wasn't aware of it, of course, it's just that somehow, she'd always felt like HIV was in another category. She was dismayed at how something so recent and devastating hadn't been the first thing she'd turned to. As of 2018, about 28.5 million people live with HIV – which, provided you have access to antiretroviral therapy, is no longer a death sentence. It's estimated that 25 million people died of AIDS from 1982–2002. Those years don't even include the peak: in 2005, over 2 million people died of HIV-related complications.

'We sipped champagne // from small black bottles, followed manicured paths / between trees that had lost their bark / and smelled like medicine' is how Joy Ladin recalls a decade during what many people call the Crisis. The AIDS epidemic was happening everywhere, but, for some, it caused little interruption. This may not have been as a result of callous disinterest, but more the fact that parts of the population imagined their lives would always be unaffected by HIV, hence it seemed ignorable for them. What this also meant was that there were delays in funding the kind of research that would eventually lead to today's antiretrovirals. HIV and coronavirus are entirely different, and many of the comparisons made between them are sloppy and poor, even dangerous. But one comparison is useful: that of attention and funding. Explicit in so much of Covid's funding priority is the recognition that this pandemic is something even the 'innocent' can get. The implications of the idea that the opposite might apply to HIV are left unstated, but nonetheless carry enormous power. HIV was often considered to be something people got through their own 'fault', and corresponding horrors were meted out to people who were suffering both from a health crisis and from structural and personal discrimination.

San Francisco was a city that could not ignore the reality of HIV in the era of this poem: 1982–1992. Joy Ladin describes what she can see: the hills, the festivals, the view towards Alcatraz, the visitors, the weather. There is light and sunshine and space in the opening stanzas, and a sense that the San Francisco she was experiencing was the San Francisco others were too: 'The views were what everyone had' then gives way to a reference to the epidemic; then goes back to champagne and manicured paths.

'Living in the Past' is a poem of reminiscence, but also a poem of apocalypse: something that pulls back a curtain, something that reveals. To look at this decade of horrific negligence – in cities like San Francisco and many others

– is also to look at the ways in which negligence thrives: by distraction, by distancing, by blaming the populations who were trying to survive what couldn't at the time be survived. Joy Ladin isn't holding herself personally responsible for the way the whole world responded to HIV, but she is holding a mirror to herself, considering what she wasn't living through, and allowing that to be the lens through which she now considers that decade. Two different realities were possible: manicured paths for some, others with a recent diagnosis 'slumped on benches'; one person feeling the cool, another dripping 'hard bright beads of sweat'; one seeing the day, another seeing stars. The language of the poem echoes the brutality of syntax from the era: *infected* for instance – seemingly innocuous terms weaponised as instruments of blame.

Who is the *you* in this poem? Mostly, I think that the *you* is a friend of Joy Ladin's, a person living with HIV in that era. 'I wish // I'd kissed you then' has, for me, the distance of memory, a kiss that isn't possible now because of the distance of death. A friend missing a friend they lost. The kiss has another possibility, though: was the speaker of the poem afraid to kiss a beloved friend living with HIV? Does this poem expose fear? This poem does not look for pity – either for the lost friend or the speaker. It seeks to tell the truth, with the benefit of time and distance and some late-arrived courage. It's not about HIV; it's about what people living with HIV had to live with.

The title of the poem can be interpreted in different ways. *You're living in the past*, someone might say to a friend who can't let go. But there's another possibility too: *living* in the past, in that particular past, depended on what you were living with, on how well you were supported, on whether what might kill you was being addressed; it depended on your visibility being respected. In this way the whimsy of the title is not whimsy at all; instead it highlights a border between those for whom the past is possible – you need to *live* in order to have a past – and those for whom a future is denied: people who remain in the past because their future wasn't valued. The band only play anthems – songs for the living, songs for ideas, songs for celebration – not laments. The trees smell like medicine, but there was not enough medicine developed in that decade to go around.

The poem observes the thriving of some in the midst of the struggle for survival of others. Tension is a thread throughout this poem, as well as many others of Joy Ladin's. She came out as transgender in midlife, and she explores questions of religion, safety and society through the lens of transition, and also through the lens of coping with other people's opinions about trans people's lives. 'Living in the Past' – written many years after the decade it references – considers all the ways in which certain experiences are heightened by forcing others to be hidden. Joy is reckoning with herself as she recollects the past. It's an extraordinary poem of power and accountability.

I have a habit, when I'm feeling awkward or self-conscious, of running the sharp edge of a fingernail along the thin skin of my thumb. It's helped when I've visited a dentist, when I've been waiting for bad news; it's helped me hold it together when I've been shouted at by bad bosses. It is a tiny pain; it doesn't make me bleed. Other times I find my mind begins to repeat a favourite word, like a mantra, like a hymn. That helps too. Language and the body can both be repositories of safety.

On Listening to Your Teacher Take Attendance

Aimee Nezhukumatathil

Breathe deep even if it means you wrinkle
your nose from the fake-lemon antiseptic

of the mopped floors and wiped-down
doorknobs. The freshly soaped necks

and armpits. Your teacher means well,
even if he butchers your name like

he has a bloody sausage casing stuck
between his teeth, handprints

on his white, sloppy apron. And when
everyone turns around to check out

your face, no need to flush red and warm.
Just picture all the eyes as if your classroom

is one big scallop with its dozens of icy blues
and you will remember that winter your family

took you to the China Sea and you sank
your face in it to gaze at baby clams and sea stars

the size of your outstretched hand. And when
all those necks start to crane, try not to forget

someone once lathered their bodies, once patted them
dry with a fluffy towel after a bath, set out their clothes

for the first day of school. Think of their pencil cases
from third grade, full of sharp pencils, a pink pearl eraser.

Think of their handheld pencil sharpener and its tiny blade.

Poems about school can sometimes require a particular kind of attention for me. Not because they're not capable of holding my attention, it's just that that word *school* is so evocative of years of my own life that I begin associating my own memories with the poem rather than reading the poem in front of me. I meet people who speak about their school years with deep gratitude and nostalgia and I wonder what planet they grew up on. I didn't have a hellish experience, but not a happy one either. See? I've already digressed. When someone writes a poem about school, I have to work hard to listen to them, not myself.

In 'On Listening to Your Teacher Take Attendance', Aimee Nezhukumatathil observes her younger self. This is a younger self who knows what it's like to be in a new classroom. The pupil coaches herself on the techniques she's learnt – or been taught – for holding yourself together while you're inhabiting that strange role: the new girl. 'Breathe deep', the first line instructs, good advice before you plunge underwater. The teacher mispronounces her name, but she tries to believe that he might mean well. Then everybody turns to look at her, and she tells herself not to blush.

How many moves does a young person need to go through in order to learn these lessons? More than one, for sure.

This is a poem about how much a young person knows, about how deep their resources can go, about how the repository the child draws on is the same one the adult draws on.

Listen to the body, the poet urges herself; *don't get upset when they mess up your name again*, she adds. Then the poem turns towards the ocean, as do many of the poems in the book that contains this one, a collection titled *Oceanic*. Aimee Nezhukumatathil has a lifelong interest in wild things, and her most recent prose book, *World of Wonders*, is a book in praise of *Fireflies, Whale Sharks and Other Astonishments.* She's been drawing sustenance from the ocean and its wonders ever since she was a child. 'Just picture all the eyes as if your classroom // is one big scallop with its dozens of icy blues', she says to herself, knowing that such memories bring back wonder, and a sense of home. Instead of feeling her face flush red, she urges herself – her body, her skin – to remember the winter trip to the 'China Sea and you sank / your face in it'.

Personhood and water combine in the remembrance that everyone in the class was once bathed and patted dry by someone older. They all had to learn to dress; they all felt scared at school once too, with new uniforms and pencils with 'a pink pearl eraser'. The child-speaker in the poem is inviting herself into a sense of ease; a sense of ease not granted – not yet – by her classmates. Her resilience is held – buoyed up – by family, and she draws on this archive of love when she's somewhere new, somewhere strange, somewhere unfriendly.

One of the things I love about this poem is how seriously Aimee takes the sense of threat in the classroom. The poem has magnificent images to depict the danger felt by the new girl in the class: the teacher, who mangles her name, is a butcher with 'handprints // on his white, sloppy apron'; the pencils have sharp points; and others in the class – craning their necks to see this girl whose name has been bloodied

– carry tiny blades in their schoolbags. Some of these are the fears of a child; some of these – oh the 'white' of that 'sloppy apron' – are the deep insights of a child being told, again, that she does not yet belong within the system that excludes her.

The wisdom of this poem is that it does not seek to respond to suspicion with suspicion. The voice in this poem reminds itself that everyone feels alone at times, even if they deny it. In the face of new awkwardness in classrooms, the speaker in this poem turns to that which sustains her: the ocean, and the family who've taken her to it. It is an inner gaze that Aimee cultivates; it is a reminiscence she holds on to. It is a tool of survival.

But this inner gaze isn't just turned towards the inward life, it also turns outwards: Aimee Nezhukumatathil stands in front of a new classroom – all those pairs of eyes trained on her – and transforms them into a single many-eyed animal. Then she thinks about how every one of them needs love; indeed, is loved, even if such tendernesses seem alien in the sharp experience of a classroom. Her self-soothing transforms her experience: the new class is a wild creature, but also in need of care. In that way, perhaps, the poem issues an invitation to its readers too: what do *you* turn to in times of fear or newness? Why?

I've disliked my appearance for as long as I can remember: early childhood experiences of being told I looked strange, or had the wrong-shaped head, an ugly chin, or too-long legs. Anything I could hate about myself I've hated. As a teenager, I sat in my bedroom and told myself I was *ugly*. Harsh language – I'm glad I did it; it was the beginning of a conversation. The word seeped into poetry I was writing. Bit by bit, parts of me I'd always been afraid of began to answer back.

Bioluminescence

Paul Tran

There's a dark so deep beneath the sea the creatures beget their own
light. This feat, this act of adaptation, I could say, is beautiful

though the creatures are hideous. Lantern fish. Hatchetfish. Viperfish.
I, not unlike them, forfeited beauty to glimpse the world hidden

by eternal darkness. I subsisted on falling matter, unaware
from where or why matter fell, and on weaker creatures beguiled

by my luminosity. My hideous face opening, suddenly, to take them
into a darkness darker and more eternal than this underworld

underwater. I swam and swam toward nowhere and nothing.
I, after so much isolation, so much indifference, kept going

even if going meant only waiting, hovering in place. So far below, so far
away from the rest of life, the terrestrial made possible by and thereby

dependent upon light, I did what I had to do. I stalked. I killed.
I wanted to feel in my body my body at work, working to stay

alive. I swam. I kept going. I waited. I found myself without meaning
to, without contriving meaning at the time, in time, in the company

of creatures who, hideous like me, had to be their own illumination.
Their own god. Their own genesis. Often we feuded. Often we fused

like anglerfish. Blood to blood. Desire to desire. We were wild. Bewildered. Beautiful in our wilderness and wildness. In the most extreme conditions

we proved that life can exist. *I exist. I am my life,* I thought, approaching at last the bottom of the sea. It wasn't the bottom. It wasn't the sea.

'Bioluminescence' wears the mantle of a nature poem, but we quickly realise that it is better understood as a poem about natures: the nature of making light and finding nurture, particularly on the ocean floor; human nature too, and the tendency in our species to dominate and exclude, to isolate and show indifference.

This poem of twenty-two lines, arranged in eleven couplets, looks at the peculiarity of fish adapted for survival in the depths. In them, and in their 'hideous' natures, Paul Tran has a lens through which to view patterns of survival. Reading down the page, a metaphorical journey of exploration unfolds: we go to the bottom of the sea; but then we go deeper – into the human condition.

With such dramatic imagery – bioluminescence, lantern fish, hatchetfish, viperfish, eternal darkness, the underworld and the underwater – it could be easy to think this poem's architecture rests upon all that cinematic brilliance. But it's the conjugation of the verbs, especially in the first person, that gives this poem its power: *I subsisted . . . I swam, I . . . kept going, I did what I had to do . . . I stalked . . . I killed . . . I wanted to feel . . . I waited . . . I found myself . . . we feuded . . . we fused . . . we were . . . we proved . . . I exist . . . I am . . . I thought . . .* These are verbs of verve and survival.

Through hideous ocean creatures Paul Tran explores desire and the drive to survive. The poem ends: 'It wasn't the bottom. It wasn't the sea.' If it wasn't the bottom, what was it then? Was it an opening into another world? A new beginning? A way of thriving, not just surviving? In Dante's *Inferno* the poet must venture down, down, down, through the nine circles of Hell, in order to emerge. This poem, too, goes down and yet, this descent is not a drowning, but a powerful expression of primal nature. With words like 'beget' and 'god' and 'genesis' this poem echoes creation myths. It takes lines like 'darkness hovered over the deep' from the book of Genesis and suggests that darkness hovered in the deep too, then plunges its readers into it.

What is this hideousness that Paul Tran speaks of? The poem is unambiguous: 'the creatures are hideous' and 'I, not unlike them, forfeited beauty', 'my hideous face opening'. The speaker of the poem is aware of how some might perceive them – hideous – but alongside this knowledge is a sense of agency, that there are 'creatures beguiled // by my luminosity'. This is a poem about banishment, but also about self-discovery on the other side of exile: 'I found myself without meaning / to, without contriving meaning at the time'. This strange discovery did not happen in isolation, but 'in the company // of creatures . . . like me'.

When I was twenty-two I went to a gay bar for the first time. It was a Sunday afternoon in Dublin and an old friend had introduced me to some gay men she knew. I was compelled, but conflicted. I repeated objections that I'd heard from religious conservatives: 'What's the need for self-separation?' 'Wait and see how it feels,' one of my new friends said. Sitting with a pint of stout in a bar where I could guess I'd be safe was an experience I'd never considered possible before. This was the 1990s, and gay bars were – in the imagination I'd been given – dens of iniquity, places of depravity. Nobody had told me how good the music was;

nobody had told me I could feel safe; nobody had told me how people looked out for each other. I was converted.

There are many remarkable things about 'Bioluminescence', but one of them is how it does not idolise community. People who've felt marginalised may often find enormous solace and delight with each other, once they've found it. Paul Tran knows that safe community will always have conflict: because nobody fights through isolation or doubt to come out unscathed; because communities made of people with scars inflict other scars; because safe conflict is an extraordinary form of play; because art thrives with electricity; because light can be made when conflict can be disarmed; because tension is a glorious thing, provided tension is not killing you. 'Often we feuded. Often we fused // like anglerfish. Blood to blood. Desire to desire. We were wild. Bewildered. // Beautiful in our wilderness and wildness.'

Anglerfish is a word that can easily – if looked at too quickly – be mistaken for angelfish or angerfish. Maybe it's all three: fishing, fury and fabulous creatures. Paul Tran, who uses they/them pronouns, is committed to looking at the multiplicities of things. Hideous is not the final word for things previously called hideous. The 'I' of this poem embraces ugliness and finds beauty in it. Beauty is its own illumination in 'Bioluminescence'. The poem ends in the deep, with the emptiness of blank space, allowing anybody reading it to read themselves, in the same way that Paul Tran has read themselves, into the lantern fish, the hatchetfish, the viperfish, the anglerfish. 'Their own god. Their own genesis.'

Notes on the Poets

Hanif Abdurraqib writes poetry, essays, and cultural criticism. He has released two collections of poetry: *The Crown Ain't Worth Much* (Button Poetry, 2016) and *A Fortune for Your Disaster* (Tin House, 2019). For the latter, he was awarded the 2020 Lenore Marshall Prize. His collection of essays, *A Little Devil in America: In Praise of Black Performance* (Random House, 2021) won the Gordon Burn Prize, was shortlisted for the National Book Award, and was named one of the best books of the year by the *New York Times*.

Patience Agbabi was elected a Fellow of the Royal Society of Literature in 2017. Her work has been featured in multiple journals and anthologies, including *The Penguin Book of New Black Writing in Britain*, and Carol Ann Duffy's 2012 collection *Jubilee Lines* (Faber & Faber). Her collection *Telling Tales* (Canongate, 2014), was shortlisted for the Ted Hughes Award for New Work in Poetry.

Dilruba Ahmed is the author of two collections of poetry: *Dhaka Dust* (Graywolf Press, 2011) and *Bring Now the Angels* (University of Pittsburgh Press, 2020). Her first collection won the Bakeless Literary Prize for Poetry; she has also been awarded the Dorothy Sargent Rosenberg

Memorial Prize, and the *Florida Review* Editors' Award. Her work was featured in *The Best American Poetry 2019* (Scribner).

Kaveh Akbar is an Iranian–American poet, born in Tehran in 1989. He is the founder of divedapper.com, a project dedicated to interviewing major voices in contemporary American poetry. His poems have appeared in *The New Yorker, The New York Times, Paris Review* and others. In 2016, he received a Lucille Medwick Memorial Award. He published his second poetry volume, *Pilgrim Bell*, with Graywolf Press in 2021.

Yehuda Amichai was a German-born Israeli poet whose work has been translated into forty languages. He received an Israel Prize for Hebrew Poetry in 1982, a Brenner Prize in 1969, and several nominations for the Nobel Prize. His poetry was included in the anthology *100 Great Poems of the Twentieth Century* (ed. Mark Strand (Faber & Faber, 2005)). He became an honorary member of the American Academy of Arts and Letters in 1986. A collection of his papers (including manuscripts, personal correspondence and journals, and written in multiple languages) is housed at the Beinecke Rare Book and Manuscript Library at Yale University.

Raymond Antrobus was born in London in 1986. For his book *The Perseverance* (Penned in the Margins, 2018), he was awarded the Rathbones Folio Prize for Best Work of Literature in Any Genre. As well as featuring in publications including *Poetry Review,* the *New Statesman* and the *Deaf Poets Society,* he has appeared at Glastonbury Festival, and in 2021 performed at the Paralympic Homecoming

Ceremony at Wembley Stadium. He won the 2019 Ted Hughes Award, and was elected a fellow of the Royal Society of Literature in 2020. His second collection, *All the Names Given* (Picador, 2021), was named one of the best poetry books of 2021 by the *Guardian.*

Margaret Atwood was born in Canada in 1939. She is the recipient of dozens of awards and honorary degrees, including the Booker Prize for *The Testaments* (McClelland & Stewart, 2019); a British Academy President's Metal, the Dayton Literary Peace Prize, and a Canadian Booksellers' Lifetime Achievement Award. Since 1961, she has published over fifty books, spanning poetry, children and adult fiction, collections of essays, and graphic novels. *Dearly*, her most recent book of poetry, was published by Chatto & Windus in 2020.

Reginald Dwayne Betts is the author of three collections of poetry. For *Bastards of the Reagan Era* (Four Way Books, 2015), he won the PEN New England Award in Poetry. He is the recipient of a Soros Justice Fellowship, a Radcliffe Fellowship, a Ruth Lilly Fellowship and a Guggenheim Fellowship. His most recent collection *Felon* (W.W. Norton, 2019) won an NAACP Image Award. He was appointed a Member of President Obama's Coordinating Council of the Office of Juvenile Justice and Delinquency Prevention. He founded Freedom Reads, an organisation providing incarcerated people with access to books.

Xochitl-Julisa Bermejo was born in California to Mexican parents. She is co-founder of Women Who Submit, an organisation that seeks to empower women and non-binary writers to put work forward for publication. In the autumn of 2017, she became the first 'Poet in the Parks' resident at Gettysburg National Military Park. Her debut poetry collection *Posada: Offerings of Witness and Refuge* (Sundress Publications) was published in 2016.

Mark S. Burrows is a poet, translator, academic, and teacher, whose work has appeared in publications including the *Anglican Theological Review,* the *Southern Quarterly* and *Almost Island.* He is the co-translator of two collections of meditations based on the writings of Meister Eckhart. His book *Prayers of a Young Poet* is an edition of translated extracts from Rainer Maria Rilke's *Book of Hours*. His poetry collection *The Chance of Home* was published by Paraclete Press in 2018.

Vahni (Anthony) Capildeo was born in Trinidad in 1973. They were awarded the University of Leeds Douglas Caster Cultural Fellowship in Poetry in 2017 and were the Seamus Heaney Centre Fellow in Poetry from 2019–2020. They were awarded the Forward Prize for their 2016 collection *Measures of Expatriation* (Carcanet Press). *Like a Tree, Walking* (Carcanet Press, 2021) was named the Poetry Book Society's Winter Choice in 2021.

Ali Cobby Eckermann is a Yankunytjatjara woman, born on Kaurna land in South Australia in 1963. Her debut collection of poetry, *Little Bit Long Time*, was published in 2009 as part of the New Poets Series of the Australian Poetry Centre. She won the Kenneth Slessor Prize for Poetry with her verse novel *Ruby Moonlight* (2012). Her fourth poetry collection, *Inside my Mother*, was published by Giramondo in 2015. In 2017, she was awarded the Windham-Campbell Prize for Poetry.

Imtiaz Dharker was born in Lahore, Pakistan, and raised in Glasgow. She is a former Poet in Residence at Cambridge University Library. She was the recipient of the Queen's Gold Medal for Poetry in 2014, and the Cholmondeley Award in 2011. Her poems are included on the national curriculum in the UK, and she has performed to audiences of students all over the country. Her most recent poetry collection, *Luck is the Hook*, was published by Bloodaxe Books in 2018.

Natalie Diaz was born in 1978 in the Fort Mojave Indian Village in Needles, California. She is a member of the Gila River Indian community. Her work has been featured in the *New Yorker*, and the Academy of American Poets' *Poem-a-Day.* She is the author of two collections of poetry: *When My Brother Was an Aztec* (Copper Canyon Press, 2012), and *Postcolonial Love Poem* (Faber & Faber 2020), which won the Pulitzer Prize. She was elected a Chancellor of the Academy of American Poets in 2021.

Martín Espada is a poet, editor, essayist, translator, professor of English, and former tenant lawyer. He is the recipient of a Ruth Lilly Poetry Prize, an Academy of American Poets Fellowship, and a Guggenheim Fellowship. His collection *The Republic of Poetry* (W.W. Norton, 2006), was a finalist for the Pulitzer Prize. His most recent book of poems, *Floaters* (W.W. Norton, 2020), won the 2021 National Book Award. He is the editor of *What Saves Us: Poems of Empathy and Outrage in the Age of Trump* (Northwestern University Press, 2019).

Kathleen Flenniken served as Washington State Poet Laureate from 2012–2014. She has been awarded a Pushcart Prize and a fellowship from the National Endowment of the Arts. She is the author of three poetry collections. *Plume* (University of Washington Press, 2012) was awarded the Washington State Book Award. Her most recent collection, *Post Romantic*, was published in 2020.

Richard Georges was born in Trinidad in 1982. He was named the first Poet Laureate of the British Virgin Islands in 2020. He is co-founder of *Moko*, an online publication focused on Caribbean art and literature. His first book of poetry, *Make Us All Islands* (Shearsman Books, 2017), was shortlisted for the Forward Prize for Best First Collection. For his most recent collection, *Epiphaneia* (Out-Spoken Press, 2019), he was awarded the 2020 OCM Bocas Prize for Caribbean Literature.

Meleika Gesa-Fatafehi (also known as Vika Mana) is a poet and rapper whose ancestry includes the Zagareb and Magaram/Dauareb tribes of Mer (Murray) Island, as well as islanders from the village of Fahefa in Tonga. They have written for publications including *Overland* and *The Big Issue.* In 2019, they were one of the ten writers chosen to take part in 'The Next Chapter' scheme from the Wheeler Centre.

Aracelis Girmay was born in 1977. She is the author of three collections of poetry: *Teeth* (Northwestern University Press, 2007), *Kingdom Animalia* (BOA Editions, 2011), and *The Black Maria* (BOA Editions, 2016). She is the recipient of a Great Lakes Colleges Association New Writers Award and an Isabella Gardner Poetry Award. She won a Whiting Award in 2015.

Lorna Goodison served as the Poet Laureate of Jamaica from 2017–2020. She has written three collections of short stories, appeared in numerous anthologies, and published a memoir,

From Harvey River: A Memoir of My Mother and Her Ireland (Atlantic Books, 2007), which won the British Columbia National Award for Canadian Non-Fiction. She is the recipient of a Windham-Campbell Literature Prize and the Queen's Gold Medal for Poetry. She published her fifteenth poetry collection, *Mother Muse*, with Carcanet in 2021.

Roshni Goyate is one of the four writers and performers who make up the collective 4 BROWN GIRLS WHO WRITE. In 2020, they published a collection of the same name with Rough Trade Books. The collection featured four pamphlets: one by each author. The group has appeared across the UK and internationally at events and venues including the Edinburgh Fringe, Tate Britain, and the Muscat Literary Festival.

Carlos Andrés Gómez has been featured in the *Irish Times*, *Button Poetry*, TEDx, *The New York Times*, *South China Morning Post* and *HuffPost Latino Voices.* His debut poetry collection, *Fractures* (University of Wisconsin Press, 2020), won the 2020 Felix Pollak Prize and the 2021 Midwest Book Award Gold Medal for Poetry. In collaboration with musician/producer Brent Shuttleworth, Carlos released a spoken word album *Opus* in August 2021. His performances of poems including 'Where are you *really* from? and 'What Latino Looks Like' have been viewed more than ten million times online.

Marie Howe was born in New York State in 1950, and served as the state's Poet Laureate from 2012–2014. She has released four collections of poetry: *The Good Thief* (Persea Books, 1988), *What the Living Do* (W.W. Norton, 1998), *The Kingdom of Ordinary Time* (W.W. Norton, 2009), and

Magdalene (W.W. Norton, 2017). *What the Living Do* was named one of the five best poetry collections of the year by *Publishers Weekly*. In 2018, she was appointed a Chancellor of the Academy of American Poets.

Ilya Kaminsky was born in 1977 in Ukraine (at that time, part of the former Soviet Union), and granted political asylum by the United States in 1993. He was named by the BBC as one of the 'twelve artists that changed the world in 2019'. His most recent poetry collection *Deaf Republic* (Graywolf Press, 2019; Faber & Faber in the UK) was named Best Book of the Year by the *Washington Post*, the *Guardian* and the *Financial Times*, among others. *Deaf Republic* also won a National Jewish Book Award. He is the co-founder of Poets for Peace, which sponsors poetry readings across the globe in support of relief work.

Rafiq Kathwari was born in the disputed Kashmir Valley. In 2013, he became the first non-Irish writer to win the Patrick Kavanagh Poetry Award. The winning collection of poems was later published as *In Another Country* (Doire Press, 2015). His most recent book of poems *My Mother's Scribe* was published with Yoda Press in 2020.

Jónína Kirton is a Red River Métis/Icelandic poet. She has released two collections of poetry with Talon Books: *page as bone ~ ink as blood* (2015), and *An Honest Woman* (2017) which was a finalist for the Dorothy Livesay Poetry Prize. She received Vancouver's Mayor's Arts Award for an Emerging Artist in the Literary Arts in 2016, at the age of sixty-one. Her third book, *Standing in a River of Time*, was released in Spring 2022.

Zaffar Kunial was the Wordsworth Trust Poet-in-Residence in 2014, publishing a pamphlet in the Faber New Poets series in the same year. He was one of four poets commissioned for the Poetry Society project The Pity, created to mark the centenary of the First World War. His first poetry collection, *Us*, was published by Faber & Faber in 2018.

Joy Ladin is a poet, essayist, literary scholar, and widely recognised speaker on transgender issues. She is the recipient of multiple accolades, including a Hadassah Brandeis Research Fellowship, a Hashamat Lev Award, two Forward Fives awards, the 'Continuing the Legacy of Stonewall' Award 2012, and a Fulbright Scholarship. She has released nine books of poetry. Her most recent, *The Future Is Trying to Tell Us Something: New and Selected Poems*, was published by Sheep Meadow Press in 2017

Ada Limón was born in California in 1976. Her work has appeared in publications including *The New Yorker* and the *Harvard Review*. Her 2018 collection *The Carrying* won the National Book Critics Circle Award for Poetry, and she was a awarded a Guggenheim Fellowship in 2020. Her most recent collection, *The Hurting Kind*, was published in May 2022.

Layli Long Soldier is a citizen of the Oglala Lakota Nation. In 2012, her participatory installation, *Whereas We Respond*, was featured on the Pine Ridge Reservation. Her work has appeared in the *American Poet* and the *American Indian Journal of Culture and Research*. Her poetry collection *Whereas* (Graywolf Press, 2017), won the National Book Critics Circle Award, and was shortlisted for the 2018 Griffin Poetry Prize.

Gail McConnell was born in Belfast in 1981. She is the author of two pamphlets of poetry: *Fothermather* (Ink Sweat & Tears, 2019) and *Fourteen* (Green Bottle Press, 2018). Her collection *The Sun Is Open* (Penned in the Margins, 2021) was a Poetry Book of the Month in the *Guardian*, a Book of the Year in the *Times Literary Supplement*, and a poetry Book of the Year in the *Irish Times*. She teaches at the Seamus Heaney Centre for Poetry at Queen's University Belfast.

Kei Miller was born in Jamaica in 1978. He was named one of the twenty Next Generation Poets by the Poetry Book Society in 2014. In the same year, he released his fourth collection of poetry. *The Cartographer Tries to Map a Way to Zion* (Carcanet, 2014) was awarded the Forward Prize for Best Collection. His most recent poetry collection *In Nearby Bushes* (Carcanet, 2019) was shortlisted for the Derek Walcott Prize, and was named a *Telegraph* Book of the Year.

Brad Aaron Modlin won the Cowles Poetry Book Prize with his debut collection *Everyone at this Party Has Two Names* (Southeast Missouri State University Press, 2016). He is also the author of *Surviving in Drought*, a collection of short stories. His work has appeared in publications including *Heavy Feather Review*, *DIAGRAM*, the *Florida Review*, and *Proximity Magazine*.

Faisal Mohyuddin's work has appeared in *Poetry* magazine, *Chicago Quarterly Review*, and *RHINO*. His collection *The Displaced Children of Displaced Children* (Eyewear Publishing, 2018) won the 2017 Sexton Prize in Poetry, and received an Honourable Mention from the Association of Asian American Studies. He is one of the twenty-three artists whose work was featured in the 2020 virtual exhibit 'American Muslim Futures'.

Aimee Nezhukumatathil's work has been featured in *New York Times Magazine* and the *American Poetry Review*. She is the author of four poetry collections; the most recent, *Oceanic*, was published by Copper Canyon Press in 2018. She is Poetry Editor for *Sierra* magazine, and was awarded a Guggenheim Fellowship in 2020. Her illustrated collection of nature essays, *World of Wonders: In Praise of Fireflies, Whale Sharks, and Other Astonishments*, was Barnes and Noble's 2020 Book of the Year.

Gregory Pardlo was born in Philadelphia in 1968. His collection *Digest* (Four Way Books, 2014) won the Pulitzer Prize for Poetry in 2015, and was nominated for the 46th NAACP Image Award for Outstanding Literary Work in Poetry, among many other accolades. He was awarded a Guggenheim Fellowship in 2017. His poems have appeared in publications such as *The New Yorker* and *American Poetry Review* as well as anthologies including the *Angles of Ascent: A Norton Anthology of Contemporary African American Poetry*.

Leanne O'Sullivan was born in Cork in 1983. In her early twenties, she won several of Ireland's poetry competitions, including the RTÉ Rattlebag Poetry Slam. She is the author of four collections of poetry. Her second, *Cailleach: The Hag of Beara* (Bloodaxe, 2009), won the Rooney Prize for Irish Literature in 2010. Her 2019 collection *A Quarter of an Hour* (Bloodaxe) won the Farmgate Café National Poetry Award, and was shortlisted for the *Irish Times* Poetry Now Award.

Yousif M. Qasmiyeh was born and educated in the Baddawi refugee camp in North Lebanon. His 2021 collection

Writing the Camp (Broken Sleep Books) was named one of the Best Poetry Books of 2021 by the *Telegraph* and the *Irish Times*, and selected as the Poetry Society 2021 Spring Recommendation. He is the Writer-in-Residence of Refugee Hosts.

Noʻu Revilla was born on the island of Maui. She released the pamphlet *Say Throne* with Tinfish Press in 2011. In 2021, she was selected as one of five winners of the annual National Poetry Series competition. *Ask the Brindled*, her debut poetry collection, was published by Milkweed Editions in 2022.

Rainer Maria Rilke was an Austrian writer of poetry, letters, and prose. His work was characterised by interests in philosophy, romanticism, lyricism, and the notion of art as the primary source of meaning. His major influences included Leo Tolstoy and Auguste Rodin. His collection *The Book of Hours* was published in three parts between 1899 and 1903.

Roger Robinson was elected a Fellow of the Royal Society of Literature in 2020. His collection *The Butterfly Hotel* (Peepal Tree Press, 2013), was shortlisted for the OCM Bocas Prize for Caribbean Literature. For *A Portable Paradise* (Peepal Tree Press, 2019), he was awarded the T. S. Eliot Poetry Prize and the Ondaatje Prize. He is co-founder of the international writing collective Malika's Poetry Kitchen.

Peggy Robles-Alvarado is the award-winning author of *Conversations with My Skin* (2011) and *Homage to the Warrior Women* (2012). Through Robleswrites Productions, she created the *Abuela Stories Project* (2016) and the 2017 anthology *Mujeres, the Magic, the Movement, and the Muse*. Her performance poetry has been featured at NYU Latinx

Caribbean Poetry Festival, Harvard University, and the Smithsonian Institute's Museum of the American Indian. In 2021, she was awarded a Jerome Hill Foundational Fellowship in Literature.

Esteban Rodríguez is the author of five poetry collections: *Dusk & Dust* (Hub City Press, 2019), *Crash Course* (Saddle Road Press, 2019), *In Bloom* (SFASU Press, 2020), *(Dis) placement* (Skull + Wind Press, 2020), and *The Valley* (Sundress Publications, 2021). His debut essay collection, *Before the Earth Devours Us*, was published by Split/Lip Press in 2021.

Lemn Sissay was born in England in 1967. He has written poetry, drama, and children's fiction, and his work has appeared at the Royal Academy and the British Film Institute. He became a trustee of London's Foundling Museum in 2017. His autobiography, *My Name is Why* (Canongate, 2019), recounts his own experience of growing up in the UK care system. The recipient of honorary doctorates from universities including Kent and Manchester, he was the official poet of the London 2012 Olympics and won the PEN Pinter Prize in 2019.

Tracy K. Smith was the United States Poet Laureate from 2017-2019. She won the 2012 Pulitzer Prize for *Life on Mars* (Graywolf Press, 2011). Her most recent collection, *Wade in the Water* (Graywolf Press, 2018) was awarded the Anisfield-Wolf Book Award for Poetry, and shortlisted for the T. S. Eliot Book Prize. *Such Colour*, a new and selected, was published in 2021.

Paul Tran's work has appeared in *The New Yorker*, the *Nation* and *Best American Poetry*. They were the first trans poet to win New York's Nuyorican Poets Café Grand Slam. They are the recipient of a Ruth Lilly & Dorothy Sargent Rosenberg Fellowship from the Poetry Foundation. Their debut collection *All the Flowers Kneeling* was published by Penguin in 2022.

Natasha Trethewey was born in Mississippi in 1966, and served as US Poet Laureate from 2012–2014. She won the Pulitzer Prize for her poetry collection *Native Guard* (Houghton Mifflin, 2006). Her memoir *Memorial Drive* (Ecco Press, 2020) became a *New York Times* bestseller and was named one of the Best Books of the Year by the *Washington Post*. In 2020, she was awarded the Rebekah Johnson Bobbitt National Prize for Poetry (lifetime achievement) from the Library of Congress.

R. A. Villanueva is a two-time winner of the *Ninth Letter* Literary Award for poetry. His work has appeared in *American Poetry Review*, *Bellevue Literary Review* and *Virginia Quarterly Review*. His 2014 book *Reliquaria* (University of Nebraska Press) won the Prairie Schooner Book Prize in Poetry. He is a founding editor of *Tongue: A Journal of Writing & Art.*

Ocean Vuong was born in Vietnam in 1988 and raised in the United States. His first collection, *Night Sky with Exit Wounds* (Copper Canyon Press, 2016) won the T. S. Eliot Prize, the Whiting Award, and a Forward Prize. He has featured in publications including the *Atlantic, Granta, The New York Times,* and the *Paris Review*. His 2020 novel *On Earth We're Briefly Gorgeous* (Vintage) was multi-award winning and became a *New York Times* bestseller. His second collection of poems, *Time Is a Mother*, was published by Penguin Press in 2022.

Christian Wiman was born in 1966. He teaches courses on Religion and Literature at Yale Divinity School, and was the editor of *Poetry* magazine from 2003 to 2013. His work has featured in publications including the *Atlantic*, *The New Yorker*, and *Harper's Magazine*. For his collection *Every Riven Thing* (Farrar, Strauss & Giroux, 2010), he won the Commonwealth Prize from the English-Speaking Union. *Survival Is a Style* was published in 2020.

James Wright was awarded the Yale Younger Poets' Prize for his first collection, *The Green Wall*, published in 1956. In 1972, he won the Pulitzer Prize for his *Collected Poems*. Nine books of his poetry were published during his lifetime; two more have been published since his death in 1980. An annual festival to celebrate his poetry took place in Martins Ferry, Ohio (his hometown), between 1981 and 2007.

Acknowledgements

Jamie Byng wrote to me one day, saying he and Silvie Varela had been listening to the Poetry Unbound podcast. He suggested – charmed! – a book partnership. Jamie, for your enthusiasm, skill, insight and brilliance, thank you. Silvie, for your ears, attention and influence, thank you. Megan Reid and Aa'Ishah Hawton at Canongate were magnificent editors, thank you. Thank you also to Lucy Zhou, Jenny Fry, Jamie Norman, Sam Bentman, Melissa Tombere, Vicki Rutherford, Rafaela Romaya, Rebecca Bonallie, Gaia Poggiogalli and Jo Lord. Thanks to Martha Sprackland for skill and checking and correction and questions. Patience Agbabi, thank you for the friendship, poetry, introductions and advice.

I couldn't have hoped for a more insightful and brilliant editor than Jill Bialosky at W.W. Norton & Company. Jill, praising your extraordinary skill feels like praising grass for being green. But I'll praise anyway. Thank you. Drew Weitman, many thanks to you and everyone else at Norton.

Working with Clare Conville as a literary agent is a joy and a privilege. Clare, for your direction and support and magnificence, I am honoured and grateful. Thanks, too, to Darren Biabowe Barnes and all at C&W Agency.

The Poetry Unbound podcast exists because of Krista Tippett. Krista has vision and depth. She understands the need for analysis and consolation, brutal truth and hope. She trusts words, and in her friendship and trust so much has grown. For joy, friendship, and collaboration, Krista, thank you.

My colleagues at On Being are magnificent. I want to thank Chris Heagle, Liliana Maria Percy Ruíz and Gautam Srikishan for the hours – and hours and hours – of joy and poetry prep. Colleen Scheck – for the combination of detail and kindness that is so perfectly you, thank you. Lucas Johnson, for the clarity of call and collaboration, thank you. Lilian Vo, Erin Colasacco, Eddie Gonzalez, and Romy Nehme, thank you. Myrna Keliher, for art and words, thank you. Thanks, too, to Zack Rose, Julie Siple, Matt Martinez, Laurén Drommerhausen, Serri Graslie, Ashley Her, Suzette Burley, April Adamson, Kristin Lin, Ben Katt, Cameron Mussar, Lillie Benowitz, Gretchen Honnold, Jhaleh Akhavan, Amy Chatelaine, Kayla Edwards, Andrea Prevost, and all the board at On Being.

I want to thank the poets for their work, their lonely craft, their daring, creative and world-making skill. Thank you. Also: the publishers, thank you for amplifying their work in the world. Thank you to teachers – theirs and mine – for the lessons in poetry, in craft, desperation, composition and intuition.

A poem can make something new happen in the life of the reader. But a poem's reader – or listener – can also make something new of a poem too. With this in mind, I want to thank, and honour, the listeners to Poetry Unbound over the past years. What company, and listening, and care, and shared lives.

Thanks to Emily Rawling for skill, brilliance, hilarity, support, amendments, careful reading and permission-seeking. Thanks to Trent Gilliss for connection and friendship. Were I to list friends, I'd never end – thankfully their love doesn't either, nor does mine. Tuesday Group and Corrymeela have been the shaping of a home and a wrestle about what it means to breathe in a world of division. Thank you. My everlasting thanks to Anya Backlund and all at Blue Flower Arts for their care, brilliance and collaboration.

Finally, to Paul Doran, m'fhear céile agus grá mo chroí. For time, support, joy and love, mo bhuíochas, mo chuisle.

Permission Credits

About On Being

Some of the proceeds from the sale of *Poetry Unbound: 50 Poems to Open Your World* go to support the ongoing work of On Being.

Poetry Unbound the podcast, presented by Pádraig Ó Tuama, began in early 2020 and is part of the On Being suite of podcasts. Each episode is a guided reflection on a single poem.

On Being is a media and public life initiative, founded and directed by Krista Tippett, an awardee of the 2014 US National Medal for Humanities. On Being takes up the great questions of meaning in twenty-first-century lives and at the intersection of spiritual inquiry, science, social healing, and the arts. What does it mean to be human, how do we want to live, and who will we be to each other?

onbeing.org